PICTORIAL CATECHISM of the METHODIST EPISCOPAL CHURCH.

The Catechism

OF THE

METHODIST EPISCOPAL CHURCH.

Numbers 1, 2, and 3,

IN ONE VOLUME,

DESIGNED FOR CONSECUTIVE STUDY IN SUNDAY SCHOOLS AND FAMILIES.

New-York:
PUBLISHED BY CARLTON & PHILLIPS,
200 MULBERRY-STREET.
1855.

Preface.

THE characteristics of this Catechism are brevity, comprehensiveness, and systematic arrangement. It is not published as a child's Catechism merely, but as the CATECHISM OF THE CHURCH, including both young and old. The answers are generally short, and the words easy; but short words have not been chosen in preference to longer ones deemed more appropriate.

While the language is studiously adapted to the comprehension of children, it is suitable to be retained in memory through life. Hence it is not proposed in other numbers of the series to change the language of the present. This is called Catechism No. 1 only for the sake of distinction. It is *the* Catechism. No. 2 is the same, with the addition of numerous Scripture proofs and illustrations printed side by side with the several questions and answers. No. 3 is designed for a series of instructions of a much higher grade.

These several Catechisms should be used in consecutive order. In the first, the task of the scholar is to learn by heart the answers to the several questions so as to repeat them verbatim, either in numerical order, or when asked at random. This having been done, the next step of the scholar will be to commit to memory the Scripture proofs of the several answers as furnished in No. 2. The instructions of No. 3 will then be in place.

The Scripture references appended to the answers of the Catechism are merely illustrative, except when preceded by quotation marks, which indicate that the text is literally copied. It will not be necessary for pupils to pay attention to them, unless their curiosity is excited to examine the fountains of religious truth.

Continued perseverance is essential to success in catechetical instruction. It is therefore earnestly recommended to parents, teachers, and ministers to review their pupils in the Catechism with frequency and regularity.

In every Sunday school there should be at least a monthly recitation of the whole Catechism, whatever other studies may be pursued.

When a school is properly prepared in advance, this recitation need not occupy more than fifteen minutes at a time. A variety of exercises may be adopted in order to render the recitation of the Catechism interesting, *e. g.*:—

1. *Recitation in concert;* in which the superintendent will ask the questions, and all the scholars respond in one voice.

2. *Recitation by classes.*—This may be practiced by asking the questions alternately of the classes in rotation, all the members of each class responding in concert; or by alternating the questions between the male and female classes; or, finally, by examining one or more of the male classes on a whole section, and then a corresponding number of female classes on the following section, and so on until the whole recitation is completed.

3. *Individual recitation.*—In order to have this style of recitation pass off with spirit, let none be allowed to participate in it who have not in their classes shown themselves perfectly familiar with every question and answer in the Catechism. Let those who are thus familiar be arranged in a row, either sitting or standing, and let the questions be rapidly but plainly asked of the several scholars in rotation, until the lesson is finished.

Whatever plan may be adopted for the recitation of the Catechism, parents, teachers, and ministers should cherish a common solicitude to have every scholar thoroughly taught in all the questions and answers.

From such a beginning it will be easy to progress with the Scripture proofs of the second series, and also with the enlarged instructions of the third.

The teaching and frequent recitation of the *baptismal covenant* found in the Appendix is particularly recommended. The recitation ought to be accompanied with suitable instructions on the nature and obligations of Christian baptism. The Lord's prayer and the ten commandments are repeated in the Appendix for the convenience of separate study and recitation. Such portions of Scripture, including the beatitudes, ought to be kept constantly familiar to every mind.

The importance of teaching the young some forms of prayer to aid and guide their devotions, is obvious. The examples given in the Appendix are progressive in their style and length. Parents and teachers will use their discretion as to which should be recommended at any particular age.

Of the sweet and simple prayer at the end, it may be sufficient to say that some of the wisest and best of men have accustomed themselves to repeat it nightly, from early childhood to the very end of their earthly pilgrimage.

Outline of Topics.

Catechism.

I. GOD.

§ 1.—HIS NATURE AND ATTRIBUTES.

WHO made you?

God.

2. *Who is God?*

The Creator of all things.

3. *What is God?*

An uncreated Spirit?

4. *Where is God?*

God is everywhere.

5. *What does God know?*

God is all-wise; he knoweth all things, even the thoughts of our hearts.—1 John iii, 20.

6. *What can God do?*

God is almighty; he doeth whatsoever he will.

7. *How long has God existed?*

God is eternal; he has lived always, and will live forever.

8. *What is the character of God?*

"God is love."—1 John iv, 8.

9. *Is God holy?*

God is holy; he hateth all workers of iniquity.—Psa. v, 5.

10. *Is God merciful?*

"The Lord is merciful and gracious, slow to anger, and plenteous in mercy."—Psa. ciii, 8.

11. *Is God just?*

The Lord is just, rewarding the righteous and punishing the wicked.

12. *Is God true?*

He is "the God of truth."—Isa. lxv, 16. He "cannot lie."—[Titus i, 2.

§ 2.—THE PERSONS OF GOD.

13. *Are there more Gods than one?*

"There is none other God but one."—1 Cor. viii, 4.

14. *Are there more persons in the Godhead than one?*

There are three persons in the Godhead, the Father, the Son, and the Holy Ghost, and these three are ONE.—1 John v, 7.

15. *Is the Father God?*

"To us there is but one God, the Father."—1 Cor. viii, 6.

16. *Is the Son God?*

Christ "is over all, God blessed forever." He is the true God.—Rom. ix, 5; 1 John v, 20.

17. *Is the Holy Ghost God?*

The Holy Ghost is "the eternal Spirit."—Heb. ix, 14.

18. *In what name are Christians baptized?*

In the name of the Holy Trinity—the Father, the Son, and the Holy Ghost.—Matt. xxviii, 19.

II. OF CREATION.

§ 1.—THE WORLD.

19. *Can you repeat the first verse of the Bible?*

"In the beginning God created the heaven and the earth."—Gen. i, 1.

20. *Does God preserve all things which he has made?*

He upholdeth all things by the word of his power. [Heb. i, 3.

§ 2.—MAN.

21. *Of what did God make man's body?*

"Of the dust of the ground."—Gen. ii, 7.

22. *How did God make man's soul?*

God "breathed into his nostrils the breath of life, and man became a living soul."—Gen. ii, 7.

23. *How do the body and soul differ?*

The body is material and mortal, the soul is spiritual and immortal.

24. *Was man created good?*

He was; God created man in his own image.—Gen. i, 27.

25. *In what did this image of God consist?*

"In righteousness and true holiness."—Eph. iv, 24.

26. *What authority was given to man at the creation?*

God gave him dominion over every living thing.—Gen. i, 28.

§ 2.—GUILT, PREVALENCE, AND CONSEQUENCES OF SIN.

33. *What evil did their sins bring upon them?*

They lost the image of God, were driven out of Eden, and became subject to pain and death.

34. *Did their sin harm any besides themselves?*

"By the offense of one, judgment came upon all men to condemnation."—Rom. v, 18.

35. *In what state are mankind born?*

In the image of fallen Adam, destitute of original righteousness.—Gen. v, 3.

36. *What are the miseries of this condition?*

All mankind being born in sin, are by nature under the wrath of God.

IV. SALVATION.

§ 1.—THE SOURCE AND GROUNDS OF SALVATION, VIZ.: THE LOVE OF GOD IN CHRIST AND REDEMPTION THROUGH CHRIST.

37. *Did God leave mankind in sin and misery?*

No; "God so loved the world, that he gave his only-begotten Son, that whosoever believeth in him should not perish, but have everlasting life."—John iii, 16.

38. *What did the Son of God do to save sinners?*

He became man, lived, suffered, died, and rose again.

§ 2.—GUILT, PREVALENCE, AND CONSEQUENCES OF SIN.

33. *What evil did their sins bring upon them?*

They lost the image of God, were driven out of Eden, and became subject to pain and death.

34. *Did their sin harm any besides themselves?*

"By the offense of one, judgment came upon all men to condemnation."—Rom. v, 18.

35. *In what state are mankind born?*

In the image of fallen Adam, destitute of original righteousness.—Gen. v, 3.

36. *What are the miseries of this condition?*

All mankind being born in sin, are by nature under the wrath of God.

IV. SALVATION.

§ 1.—THE SOURCE AND GROUNDS OF SALVATION, VIZ.: THE LOVE OF GOD IN CHRIST AND REDEMPTION THROUGH CHRIST.

37. *Did God leave mankind in sin and misery?*

No; "God so loved the world, that he gave his only-begotten Son, that whosoever believeth in him should not perish, but have everlasting life."—John iii, 16.

38. *What did the Son of God do to save sinners?*

He became man, lived, suffered, died, and rose again.

39. *How did he become man?*

Christ, though God, took upon him the form of a servant, and was made in the likeness of man, having a human body and soul.

40. *What example does Christ's life afford us?*

An example of perfect goodness and holiness.

41. *What did Christ suffer for us?*

"He humbled himself and became obedient unto death, even the death of the cross." [Phil. ii, 8.

42. *Why did Christ thus suffer and die?*

To offer to divine justice full atonement for the sins of the world.

43. *How are we benefited by Christ's resurrection?*

He rose for our justification, and ascended to the right hand of God, where he ever liveth to make intercession for us.—Rom. iv, 25; Eph. i, 20; Col. iii, 1; Heb. vii, 25.

44. *Did Christ make this atonement for all mankind?*

By the grace of God he tasted death for every man.—Heb. ii, 9.

§ 2.—CONDITIONS OF SALVATION.

45. *Will all men therefore be saved?*

No; "The wicked shall be turned into hell, and all the nations that forget God."—Psa. ix, 17.

46. *Will those be saved who die in childhood, before they know good and evil?*

They will; for Jesus said, "Of such is the kingdom of heaven." [Matt. xix, 14.

47. *On what terms are those saved who know good from evil?*

On condition of "repentance toward God and faith toward our Lord Jesus Christ."—Acts xx, 21.

48. *What is repentance?*

A godly sorrow on account of sin.—2 Cor. vii, 10.

49. *How is true repentance indicated?*

By the forsaking of sin and a sincere turning to God.

50. *What is faith in Jesus Christ?*

Faith in Jesus Christ is the act of receiving, and trusting in him alone for salvation.—John i, 12; Phil. iii, 9.

51. *Can we repent and believe of ourselves?*

No; the power to repent and believe is given us of God.—[Eph. ii, 8; Rom. xi, 29.

52. *How can we know when we believe in Jesus Christ?*

"He that believeth on the Son of God hath the witness in himself."—1 John v, 10.

53. *What witness is this?*

"The Spirit itself beareth witness with our spirit, that we are the children of God."—Rom. viii, 16.

§ 3.—THE FRUITS AND EXTENT OF SALVATION.

54. *What fruits doth this faith produce?*

Justification, regeneration, sanctification.—Rom. v, 1; John i, 12, 13; Gal. ii, 16; 2 Thess. ii, 13.

55. *What is justification?*

Justification is that act of God's free grace in which he pardons our sins and accepts us as righteous in his sight for the sake of Christ.—Eph. i, 7; 2 Cor. v, 21; Rom. iii, 24; v, 19.

56. *What is regeneration?*

It is the new birth of the soul in the image of Christ, whereby we become the children of God.—Eph. i, 5; John i, 12, 13; John iii, 3; Eph. iv, 24; 1 John iii, 2.

57. *What is sanctification?*

Sanctification is that act of divine grace whereby we are made holy.—1 Thess. v, 23; Eph. i, 4; Col. i, 22; Heb. xiii, 12.

58. *May every believer be wholly sanctified in this life?*

Yes; God's command is, "Be ye holy, for I am holy;"

and his promise is, that "if we confess our sins" he will "cleanse us from all unrighteousness."—1 Peter i, 16; 1 Thess. iv, 8; 1 John i, 9.

59. *What is implied in being a perfect Christian, or in being wholly sanctified?*

Loving God with all our heart and soul, mind and strength, and our neighbor as ourselves.

60. *Is it possible for a justified or a sanctified Christian to fall from grace and perish?*

It is; for even the apostle Paul feared lest, after having preached to others, he himself should be a castaway.—[1 Cor. ix, 27.

61. *How shall we guard against the danger of falling from grace?*

By watchfulness, prayer, and a life of faith in the Son of God.

V. THE MEANS OF GRACE.

§ 1.—THE CHURCH AND MINISTRY.

62. *What are the principal means of grace?*

The Church, the sacraments, the word of God, and prayer.

63. *In what two forms does the Church of God exist?*

The visible and the invisible.

64. *What is the visible Church?*

The visible Church of Christ is a congregation of faithful men, in which the pure word of God is preached and the sacraments duly administered according to Christ's ordinance. [Acts ii, 42; Matt. xvi, 18; Eph. v, 27.

65. *What is the invisible Church?*

The whole body of God's true people in every period of time.

66. *Ought not all persons, where the gospel is preached, to become believers in Christ and members of the Church?*

They ought; in order to have a visible union with Christ, the Head of the Church, and communion with his people.— [Eph. v, 23; John xvii, 21; 1 Cor. xii, 20.

67. *Who are to preach the word of God and administer the sacraments?*

Faithful men, called of God and set apart by the Church to the office and work of the ministry.—Heb. v, 4; Acts xii, 2, 3; 1 Tim. iv, 14.

§ 2.—THE SACRAMENTS.

68. *How many sacraments has Christ ordained in his Church?*

Two; baptism and the Lord's supper.—Matt. xxviii, 19; 1 Cor. xi, 23–26.

69. *What is a sacrament?*

An outward and visible sign of an inward and spiritual grace.

(1.) BAPTISM.

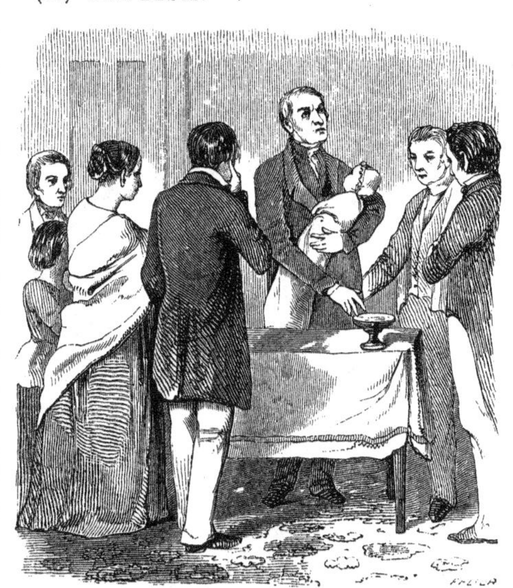

70. *What is the outward sign in baptism?*

Water, applied in the name of the Father, and of the Son, and of the Holy Ghost.—[John iii, 5; Matt. xxviii, 19.

71. *What is the inward grace signified in baptism?*

A death unto sin and a new birth unto righteousness.

72. *What advantages are secured to baptized persons?*

They are admitted to the visible Church of Christ; their

relation to him as the Mediator of the new covenant, and their title to the spiritual blessings thereto belonging, are solemnly confirmed.

(2.) THE LORD'S SUPPER.

73. *Why was the sacrament of the Lord's supper ordained?*

For the continual remembrance of the sacrifice of Christ's death, and of the benefits that we thereby receive.—1 Cor. xi, 23–26.

74. *What is the outward sign of the Lord's supper?*

Bread and wine, received according to Christ's command.

75. *What is the inward grace of this sacrament?*

The communion of the body and blood of Christ, whereby we are reminded of his sacrificial death, and spiritually strengthened to do HIS will.

§ 3.—THE WORD OF GOD AND PRAYER.

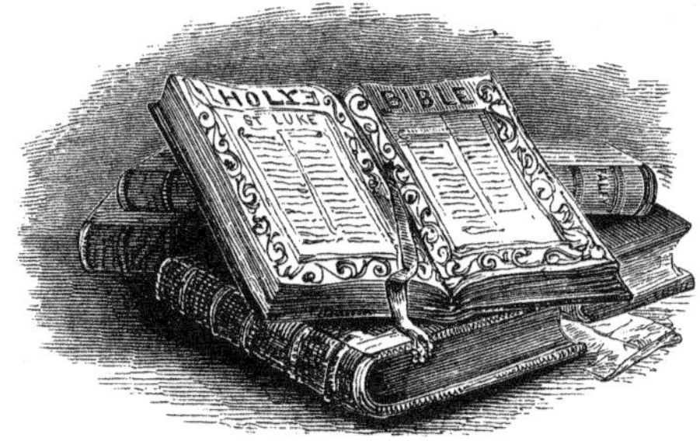

76. *Whence do we derive all correct knowledge of religious truth and duty?*

From the Holy Bible.

77. *What is the Bible?*

It is the revelation of divine truth, and the record of God's will.

78. *What is the only sufficient rule of a Christian's faith and practice?*

The word of God, as contained in the Scriptures of the Old and New Testaments.

79. *How should we use the Scriptures?*

We should seriously and diligently study God's holy word with prayer, that we may understand, believe, and practice the same.—John v, 39.

80. *What is prayer?*

Prayer is the offering up of our desires unto God in the name of Christ.

81. *With what should prayer be always accompanied?*

With humble confession of sin, with hearty thanksgiving for God's mercies, and sincere faith in his promises.

82. *Where should we offer up our prayers?*

Publicly in the house of God, and privately in our families and in our closets.

83. *What special example of prayer is given us in Scripture?*

The Lord's prayer.

84. *Can you repeat the Lord's prayer?*

Our Father which art in heaven, hallowed be thy name. Thy kingdom come. Thy will be done in earth as it is in heaven. Give us this day our dayly bread: and forgive us our trespasses, as we forgive them that trespass against us. And lead us not into temptation; but deliver us from evil: for thine is the kingdom, and the power, and the glory, forever. Amen.

VI. GOD'S LAW.

DUTIES TO GOD AND MAN.

85. *What does God require of man?*

Obedience to his revealed will.

86. *What is the rule of our obedience?*

The moral law.

87. *Where is the moral law given?*

In the ten commandments.—Exod. xx.

88. *What is the first commandment?*

Thou shalt have no other gods before me.

89. *What is the second commandment?*

Thou shalt not make unto thee any graven image, or any likeness of anything that is in heaven above, or that is in the earth beneath, or that is in the water under the earth: thou

[AN IDOL WORSHIPED BY HEATHEN.]

shalt not bow down thyself to them, nor serve them: for I the Lord thy God am a jealous God, visiting the iniquity of the fathers upon the children unto the third and fourth generation of them that hate me; and showing mercy unto thousands of them that love me, and keep my commandments.

90. *What is the third commandment?*

Thou shalt not take the name of the Lord thy God in vain: for the Lord will not hold him guiltless that taketh his name in vain.

91. *What is the fourth commandment?*

Remember the Sabbath-day, to keep it holy. Six days shalt thou labor, and do all thy work: but the seventh day is the Sabbath of the Lord thy God: in it thou shalt not do any work, thou, nor thy son, nor thy daughter, thy man-servant, nor thy maid-servant, nor thy cattle, nor thy stranger that is within thy gates: for in six days the Lord made heaven and earth, the sea, and all that in them is, and rested the seventh day: wherefore the Lord blessed the Sabbath-day, and hallowed it.

92. *What is the fifth commandment?*

Honor thy father and thy mother; that thy days may be long upon the land which the Lord thy God giveth thee.

93. *What is the sixth commandment?*

Thou shalt not kill.

94. *What is the seventh commandment?*

Thou shalt not commit adultery.

95. *What is the eighth commandment?*

Thou shalt not steal.

96. *What is the ninth commandment?*

Thou shalt not bear false witness against thy neighbor.

97. *What is the tenth commandment?*

Thou shalt not covet thy neighbor's house, thou shalt not covet thy neighbor's wife, nor his man-servant, nor his maid-servant, nor his ox, nor his ass, nor anything that is thy neighbor's.

98. *What is our Saviour's summary of God's commandments?*

He said: "Thou shalt love the Lord thy God with all thy heart, and with all thy soul, and with all thy mind. This is the first and great commandment. And the second is like unto it, Thou shalt love thy neighbor as thyself. On these two commandments hang all the law and the prophets."—Matt. xxii, 37-40.

99. *How does our Saviour explain the commandments?*

He teaches that they not only forbid sin in act, but in thought.—Matt. v, 21, 22, 27, 28.

100. *What is our Lord's precept, commonly called the golden rule?*

"Whatsoever ye would that men should do to you, do ye even so to them."—Matt. vii, 12.

101. *Can any man be saved by keeping the law?*

No; "By the deeds of the law shall no flesh be justified." [Rom. iii, 20.

102. *What then is the use of the law?*

It serves to show men their need of Christ; "For by the law is the knowledge of sin."—Rom. iii, 20; Gal. iii, 19.

103. *Are all Christians under obligation to keep the law?*

Yes; they are "not without law to God, but under the law to Christ."—1 Cor. ix, 21.

VII. OF DEATH, JUDGMENT, AND ETERNITY.

104. *Do we remain long in this world?*

No; life is short and uncertain, and we all must die.—[Job xiv, 10.

105. *Is it not a fearful thing to die?*

It is to all but true Christians.

106. *Why should not true Christians fear to die?*

Because the sting of death is removed, and they know that they shall go to heaven.

107. *How long will the bodies of men lie in the grave?*

Until the last day, when Christ shall come to raise the dead for judgment.

108. *Will all the dead be raised?*

"There shall be a resurrection of the dead, both of the just and unjust."—Acts xxiv, 15; John v, 28, 29.

109. *Will all men be judged at the last day?*

"We must all appear before the judgment seat of Christ; that *every one* may receive the things done in his body, according to that he hath done, whether it be good or bad."—2 Cor. v, 10.

110. *What sentence will Christ pronounce on the wicked?*

"Depart from me, ye cursed, into everlasting fire, prepared for the devil and his angels."—Matt. xxv, 41.

2*

111. *What will he say to the righteous?*

"Come, ye blessed of my Father, inherit the kingdom prepared for you from the foundation of the world."—Matt. xxv, 34.

112. *What will then take place?*

The world shall be destroyed by fire; and the wicked shall go away into everlasting punishment, but the righteous into life eternal.—Matt. xxv, 46; 2 Pet. iii, 10.

Appendix.

I. THE BEATITUDES.

Blessed are the poor in spirit: for theirs is the kingdom of heaven.

Blessed are they that mourn: for they shall be comforted.

Blessed are the meek: for they shall inherit the earth.

Blessed are they which do hunger and thirst after righteousness: for they shall be filled.

[THE BURNING OF MARTYRS.]

Blessed are the merciful: for they shall obtain mercy.

Blessed are the pure in heart: for they shall see God.

Blessed are the peace-makers: for they shall be called the children of God.

Blessed are they which are persecuted for righteousness' sake: for theirs is the kingdom of heaven.

[Matt. v, 3–10.

II. THE LORD'S PRAYER.

Our Father which art in heaven, hallowed be thy name. Thy kingdom come. Thy will be done in earth as it is in heaven. Give us this day our dayly bread. And forgive us our trespasses, as we forgive them that trespass against us. And lead us not into temptation, but deliver us from evil. For thine is the kingdom, and the power, and the glory, forever. *Amen.*

III. THE TEN COMMANDMENTS.

I. Thou shalt have no other gods before me.

II. Thou shalt not make unto thee any graven image, or any likeness of anything that is in heaven above, or that is in the earth beneath, or that is in the water under the earth: thou shalt not bow down thyself to them, nor serve them: for I the Lord thy God am a jealous God, visiting the iniquity of the fathers upon the children unto the third and fourth generation of them that hate me; and showing mercy unto thousands of them that love me, and keep my commandments.

III. Thou shalt not take the name of the Lord thy God in vain: for the Lord will not hold him guiltless that taketh his name in vain.

IV. Remember the Sabbath-day to keep it holy. Six days shalt thou labor, and do all thy work: but the seventh day is the Sabbath of the Lord thy God: in it thou shalt not do any work, thou, nor thy son, nor thy daughter, thy man-servant, nor thy maid-servant, nor thy cattle, nor thy stranger that is within thy gates: for in six days the Lord made heaven and

earth, the sea and all that in them is, and rested the seventh day: wherefore the Lord blessed the Sabbath-day, and hallowed it.

V. Honor thy father and thy mother; that thy days may be long upon the land which the Lord thy God giveth thee.

VI. Thou shalt not kill.

VII. Thou shalt not commit adultery.

VIII. Thou shalt not steal.

IX. Thou shalt not bear false witness against thy neighbor.

X. Thou shalt not covet thy neighbor's house, thou shalt not covet thy neighbor's wife, nor his man-servant, nor his maid-servant, nor his ox, nor his ass, nor anything that is thy neighbor's.

IV. THE APOSTLES' CREED.

I BELIEVE in God the Father Almighty, Maker of heaven and earth; and in Jesus Christ his only Son our Lord; who was conceived by the Holy Ghost, born of the Virgin Mary, suffered under Pontius Pilate; was crucified, dead, and buried; the third day he rose from the dead; he ascended into heaven, and sitteth on the right hand of God the Father Almighty; from thence he shall come to judge the quick and the dead.

I believe in the Holy Ghost; the holy catholic Church;* the communion of saints; the forgiveness of sins; the resurrection of the body, and the life everlasting. *Amen.*

* By the holy catholic Church is meant the Church of God in general.

V. BAPTISMAL COVENANT.

I renounce the devil and all his works, the vain pomp and glory of the world, with all covetous desires of the same, and the sinful desires of the flesh, so that I will not follow nor be led by them.

I believe in God the Father Almighty, Maker of heaven and earth; and in Jesus Christ his only Son our Lord; who was conceived by the Holy Ghost, born of the Virgin Mary, suffered under Pontius Pilate; was crucified, dead, and buried; the third day he rose from the dead; he ascended into heaven, and sitteth on the right hand of God the Father Almighty; from thence he shall come to judge the quick and the dead.

I believe in the Holy Ghost; the holy catholic Church; the communion of saints; the forgiveness of sins; the resurrection of the body, and the life everlasting. *Amen.*

Having been baptized in this faith, I will obediently keep God's holy will and commandments, and walk in the same all the days of my life, God being my helper.

EXAMPLES OF PRAYER FOR THE YOUNG.

MORNING PRAYER.

Almighty God, my heavenly Father, I thank thee that thou hast taken care of me the past night, and that I am alive and well this morning. Save me, O God, from evil all this day; and may I love and serve thee always. Bestow on me, I pray thee, every good thing which I need for my body and soul: assist me by thy Holy Spirit to do thy will: make me always afraid to offend thee, and let me live in thy fear and die in thy favor, and at last be saved in heaven, for Christ's sake. *Amen.*

EVENING PRAYER.

O Lord God, who knowest all things, thou seest me by night as well as by day. I pray thee, for Christ's sake, forgive me whatever I have done amiss this day, and keep me safe all night. Bless, I beseech thee, all my friends;* do good to them at all times and in all places, and help me always to serve them in love. And when I have done thy will here, by thy grace assisting me, may I be fully prepared for death and the world to come, through Christ my blessed Saviour and Redeemer. *Amen.*

* Here mention father and mother, and others.

MORNING PRAYER.

O Lord, I give thee thanks, that thou hast kept me during the night, and brought me to see another morning. Help me to pass this day in thy fear, and to remember that thine eye is always upon me; that thou hearest all I say, seest all I do, and knowest all that is in my thoughts. I confess before thee, O God, that I am a sinful creature. I have often been foolish and disobedient, and I deserve to be punished for my sins. But thou, O Lord, art merciful; thou hast promised pardon to those who repent and believe in Jesus Christ. Be merciful to me, I pray thee, and pardon my transgressions. Give me true and deep repentance for my sins, and cause me to hate every evil way. Create in me a clean heart, and renew a right spirit within me. Help me to believe, with my whole heart, in Jesus Christ, and to commit my soul to thy mercy through him. O righteous Father, grant me thy Holy Spirit to dwell within me. May he instruct, sanctify, and preserve me to the kingdom of Jesus! Be thou gracious to all my friends and enemies, and have mercy on all those who are dead in sin, and save them with me and with all for whom I should pray, for Jesus Christ's sake. *Amen.*

EVENING PRAYER.

O God, I bow down before thee, and would lift up my soul in thanksgiving for all the favors of another day. I implore thy tender mercies in the forgiveness of all my sins of thought, word, or deed, since the morning. Pardon me, O Lord, for the sake of Jesus Christ, who died upon the cross for sinners, and adopt me into thy family as one of thy children. May thy Spirit be poured down upon me! May he shed thy love abroad in my heart, and fill my mind with all good thoughts! May he teach me to love thy word, thy people, and thy house! May he help me to honor my parents, my minister, and my teachers, and to profit from their instructions! May he make me wise unto salvation, and prepare me for eternity! If I die young, may I be found ready, being washed from my sins in Jesus's blood! I ask the same mercies for all my friends. Watch over us during this night. Preserve and bless us, and let no evil come near our dwelling. May we be refreshed by rest, and awake in the morning to thy service! Grant likewise, O blessed Lord, that when days and nights with us have ended, we may sleep in Jesus, and awake in the morning of the resurrection, to join the redeemed of the Lord, and spend an eternal day in thy presence, service, and praise, for his sake! *Amen.*

MORNING PRAYER FOR THE LORD'S DAY,

TO BE ADDED TO THE USUAL MORNING PRAYER.

Suffer me not, O Lord, to waste this thy day in sin and folly; but let me worship thee with much delight. May I love thy word and thy house. Teach me to know more of thee, and to serve thee better than I have ever done before. To this end may I love my Sabbath school, and diligently improve all my opportunities to become wise unto salvation. Enable me, O Lord, to seek thee while thou mayest be found, and to call upon thee while thou art near. Thus, my Father in heaven, may I be fitted, through the merits and grace of the Lord Jesus Christ, to reign with thee in thy blessed kingdom, and to thy great name shall be the glory, world without end. *Amen.*

EVENING PRAYER FOR THE LORD'S DAY,

TO BE ADDED TO THE USUAL EVENING PRAYER.

O most gracious God, let me never forget the many good things that I have heard this day; but let them abide in my heart so that I may amend my life, and be able to give a good account of all my privileges at the judgment of the great day. May I have a heart to pity the many heathen that have no Sabbath, and a disposition to labor and pray that the gospel may be preached to all the world. Finally, when time shall end, may I be admitted to the Sabbath of rest in heaven, and give glory to the Father, the Son, and the Holy Ghost forever. *Amen.*

A SHORT PRAYER ON RETIRING TO REST.

Now I lay me down to sleep,
I pray the Lord my soul to keep;
And if I die before I wake,
I pray the Lord my soul to take.

Note to Catechism with Proofs.

DURING the study of the Catechism with proofs, no time nor trouble should be spared in making it thorough, since an accurate memorizing of leading passages of Scripture in appropriate connections is a most important object of catechetical instruction.

Every child ought to be so familiar with the principal proofs of each answer in the Catechism as to be able to recite them promptly on any occasion, and in any order. In this way habits of mental association may be formed which will be of the greatest value in after life.

Although the remarks on recitation in concert in the preface apply more especially to the Catechism proper, yet judicious and skillful teachers will be able to apply the system, in a greater or less degree, to the recitation of proofs.

The teaching and frequent recitation of the *baptismal covenant* with proofs, as found in the Appendix, is particularly recommended. The recitation ought also to be accompanied with suitable instructions on the nature and obligations of Christian baptism.

It should not be considered important, especially in the *first* study of No. 2, to learn *all* the proofs. Indeed, for young children generally, it may be quite sufficient to learn from one to three of the proofs deemed most pertinent to each question and answer. In the preparation of the Catechism it was necessary to furnish a complete selection; the number to be committed to memory may be determined by judicious parents and teachers according to the capacities of the pupil.

Catechism, with Proofs.

I. GOD.

§ 1.—HIS NATURE AND ATTRIBUTES.

1. *Who made you?*

God.

So God created man in his own image. *Gen.* 1 : 27. Thy hands have made me and fashioned me. *Psa.* 119 : 73. I have made the earth, and created man upon it. *Isa.* 45 : 12.

2. *Who is God?*

The Creator of all things.

Thou, even thou, art Lord alone; thou hast made heaven, the heaven of heavens, with all their host, the earth, and all things that are therein, the seas, and all that is therein. *Neh.* 9 : 6. God, who created all things by Jesus Christ. *Eph.* 3 : 9. All things were created by him, and for him. *Col.* 1 : 16. Thou hast created all things, and for thy pleasure they are and were created. *Rev.* 4 : 11.

3. *What is God?*

An uncreated Spirit.

The Spirit of God moved upon the face of the waters. *Gen.* 1 : 2. And God said unto Moses, I AM THAT I AM: and he said, Thus shalt thou say unto the children of Israel, I AM hath sent me unto you. *Exod.* 3 : 14. God is a Spirit. *John* 4 : 24.

4. *Where is God?*

God is everywhere.

Behold the heaven and heaven of heavens cannot contain thee. 1 *Kings*

8 : 27. Whither shall I go from thy Spirit? or whither shall I flee from thy presence? If I ascend up into heaven, thou art there: if I make my bed in hell, behold, thou art there. If I take the wings of the morning, and dwell in the uttermost parts of the sea; even there shall thy hand lead me, and thy right hand shall hold me. *Psa.* 139 : 7–10. Am I a God at hand, saith the Lord, and not a God afar off? *Jer.* 23 : 23. Do not I fill heaven and earth? saith the Lord. *Jer.* 23 : 24.

5. *What does God know?*

God is all-wise; he knoweth all things, even the thoughts of our hearts.—1 John 3 : 20.

God is mighty in strength and wisdom. *Job* 36 : 5. Thou knowest my down-sitting and mine up-rising, thou understandest my thought afar off.

Thou compassest my path and my lying down, and art acquainted with all my ways. For there is not a word in my tongue, but lo, O Lord, thou knowest it altogether. *Psa.* 139 : 2–4. Now are we sure that thou knowest all things. *John* 16 : 30. Lord, thou knowest all things. *John* 21 : 17. O the depth of the riches both of the wisdom and knowledge of God! *Rom.* 11 : 33.

6. *What can God do?*

God is almighty; he doeth whatsoever he will.

Then Job answered the Lord and said, I know that thou canst do everything. *Job* 42 : 2. Power belongeth unto God. *Psa.* 62 : 11. But our God is in the heavens: he hath done whatsoever he pleased. *Psa.* 115 : 3. Whatsoever the Lord pleased, that did he in heaven, and in earth, in the seas, and all deep places. *Psa.* 135 : 6. Behold, I am the Lord, the God of all flesh: is there anything too hard for me? *Jer.* 32 : 27. With God all things are possible. *Mark* 10 : 27. He is able even to subdue all things unto himself. *Phil.* 3 : 21. The Lord God omnipotent reigneth. *Rev.* 19 : 6.

7. *How long has God existed?*

God is eternal; he has lived always, and will live forever.

But the Lord shall endure forever. *Psa.* 9 : 7. Before the mountains were brought forth, or ever thou hadst formed the earth and the world, even from everlasting to everlasting, thou art God. *Psa.* 90 : 2. Thy years are throughout all generations. *Psa.* 102 : 24. Before me there was no God formed. *Isa.* 43 : 10. The high and lofty One that inhabiteth eternity. *Isa.* 57 : 15. I am Alpha and Omega, the beginning and the ending, saith the Lord, which is, and which was, and which is to come. *Rev.* 1 : 8.

8. *What is the character of God?*

God is love.—1 John 4 : 8.

The Lord hath appeared of old unto me, saying, Yea, I have loved thee with an everlasting love. *Jer.* 31 : 3. God so loved the world that he gave his only-begotten Son, that whosoever believeth in him should not perish, but have everlasting life. *John* 3 : 16. The God of love and peace shall be with you. 2 *Cor.* 13 : 11. God is love: and he that dwelleth in love, dwelleth in God, and God in him. 1 *John* 4 : 16.

[MURDER BY DUELLING.]

9. *Is God holy?*

God is holy; he hateth all workers of iniquity. [Psa. 5 : 5.

Worship at his footstool; for he is holy. *Psa.* 99 : 5. The Lord our God is holy. *Psa.* 99 : 9. The Lord is righteous in all his ways, and holy in all his works. *Psa.* 145 : 17. God judgeth the righteous, and God is angry with the wicked every day. *Psa.* 7 : 11. God, that is holy, shall be sanctified in righteousness. *Isa.* 5 : 16. Thou art of purer eyes than to behold evil, and canst not look on iniquity. *Hab.* 1 : 13. Who shall not fear thee, O Lord, and glorify thy name? for thou only art holy. *Rev.* 15 : 4.

10. *Is God merciful?*

The Lord is merciful and gracious, slow to anger, and plenteous in mercy.—Psa. 103 : 8.

Unto thee, O Lord, belongeth mercy. *Psa.* 62 : 12. Great are thy tender mercies, O Lord. *Psa.* 119 : 156. Thy mercy, O Lord, endureth forever. *Psa.* 138 : 8. It is of the Lord's mercies that we are not consumed, because his compassions fail not. *Lam.* 3 : 22. Though he cause grief, yet will he have compassion according to the multitude of his mercies. *Lamentations* 3 : 32. The Father of mercies and the God of all comfort. 2 *Corinthians* 1 : 3. God, who is rich in mercy. *Ephesians* 2 : 4. According to his mercy he saved us. *Titus* 3 : 5. The Lord is very pitiful, and of tender mercy. *James* 5 : 11.

11. *Is God just?*

The Lord is just, rewarding the righteous and punishing the wicked.

Thou art just in all that is brought upon us; for thou hast done right, but we have done wickedly. *Neh.* 9 : 33. Doth God pervert judgment? or doth the Almighty pervert justice? *Job* 8 : 3. He is excellent in power, and in judgment, and in plenty of justice. *Job* 37 : 23. Justice and judgment are the habitation of thy throne. *Psa.* 89 : 14. There is no God else beside me; a just God and a Saviour. *Isa.* 45 : 21. The just Lord is in the midst thereof. *Zeph.* 3 : 5. He is faithful and just to forgive us our sins. 1 *John* 1 : 9. Just and true are thy ways, thou King of saints. *Rev.* 15 : 3.

12. *Is God true?*

He is the God of truth.—Isa. 65 : 16. He cannot lie.—[Titus 1 : 2.

God is not a man, that he should lie. *Num.* 23 : 19. A God of truth and without iniquity, just and right is he. *Deut.* 32 : 4. Thou, O Lord, art a God full of compassion and gracious; long-suffering, and plenteous in mercy and truth. *Psa.* 86 : 15. Mercy and truth shall go before thy face. *Psa.* 89 : 14. The Lord is good, his mercy is everlasting; and his truth endureth to all generations. *Psa.* 100 : 5. It was impossible for God to lie. *Heb.* 6 : 18.

[DEATH OF ANANIAS AND SAPPHIRA.]

§ 2.—THE PERSONS OF GOD.

13. *Are there more Gods than one?*

There is none other God but one.—1 Cor. 8 : 4.

Hear, O Israel: the Lord our God is one Lord. *Deut.* 6 : 4. Is there a God beside me? yea, there is no God; I know not any. *Isa.* 44 : 8. I am the Lord, and there is none else, there is no God beside me. *Isa.* 45 : 5. I am God, and there is none else. *Isa.* 46 : 9. To us there is but one God. 1 *Cor.* 8 : 6. God is one. *Gal.* 3 : 20. One God and Father of all. *Eph.* 4 : 6. Thou believest that there is one God; thou doest well. *James* 2 : 19.

14. *Are there more persons in the Godhead than one?*

There are three persons in the Godhead—the Father, the Son, and the Holy Ghost, and these three are ONE.—1 John 5 : 7.

I and my Father are one. *John* 10 : 30. He that hath seen me hath seen the Father. *John* 14 : 9. The Comforter, which is the Holy Ghost, whom the Father will send in my name. *John* 14 : 26. When the Comforter is come, whom I will send unto you from the Father, even the Spirit of truth, which proceedeth from the Father, he shall testify of me. *John* 15 : 26. O Father, glorify thou me with thine own self, with the glory which I had with thee before the world was. *John* 17 : 5. While Peter thought on the vision, the Spirit said unto him. *Acts* 10 : 19. Grieve not the Holy Spirit of God, whereby ye are sealed. *Eph.* 4 : 30.

(See proofs of the three following answers.)

15. *Is the Father God?*

To us there is but one God, the Father.—1 Cor. 8 : 6.

The eternal God. *Deut.* 33 : 27. That men may know that thou, whose name alone is JEHOVAH, art the Most High over all the earth. *Psa.* 83 : 18. Have we not all one Father? hath not one God created us? *Mal.* 2 : 10. One God and Father of all. *Eph.* 4 : 6. To them that are sanctified by God the Father. *Jude* 1.

16. *Is the Son God?*

Christ is over all, God blessed forever. He is the true God.—Rom. 9 : 5; 1 John 5 : 20.

Unto us a child is born, unto us a son is given, and the government shall be upon his shoulder; and his name shall be called Wonderful, Counselor, The mighty God, The everlasting Father, The Prince of Peace. *Isa.* 9 : 6. They shall call his name Emmanuel, which, being interpreted, is, God with us. *Matt.* 1 : 23. In the beginning was the Word, and the Word was with God, and the Word was God. *John* 1 : 1. Christ Jesus: who, being in the form of God, thought it not robbery to be equal with God. *Phil.* 2 : 5, 6. For in him dwelleth all the fullness of the Godhead bodily. *Col.* 2 : 9. God was manifest in the flesh. 1 *Tim.* 3 : 16. Adorn the doctrine of God our Saviour. *Titus* 2 : 10. Unto the Son he saith, Thy throne, O God, is forever and ever. *Heb.* 1 : 8. Hereby perceive we the love of God, because he laid down his life for us. 1 *John* 3 : 16.

17. *Is the Holy Ghost God?*

The Holy Ghost is the eternal Spirit.—Heb. 9 : 14.

The Spirit of God moved upon the face of the waters. *Gen.* 1 : 2. The Spirit of God hath made me. *Job* 33 : 4. Whither shall I go from thy Spirit? *Psa.* 139 : 7. The Comforter, which is the Holy Ghost, whom the

Father will send in my name, he shall teach you all things. *John* 14 : 26. Peter said, Ananias, why hath Satan filled thy heart to lie to the Holy Ghost? . . . . Thou hast not lied unto men, but unto God. *Acts* 5 : 3, 4.

18. *In what name are Christians baptized?*

In the name of the Holy Trinity—the Father, the Son, and the Holy Ghost.—Matt. 28 : 19.

Go ye therefore, and teach all nations, baptizing them in the name of the Father, and of the Son, and of the Holy Ghost. *Matt.* 28 : 19. The grace of the Lord Jesus Christ, and the love of God, and the communion of the Holy Ghost, be with you all. 2 *Cor.* 13 : 14.

II. CREATION.

§ 1.—THE WORLD.

19. *Can you repeat the first verse of the Bible?*

In the beginning God created the heaven and the earth.—[Gen. 1 : 1.

20. *Does God preserve all things which he has made?*

He upholdeth all things by the word of his power.—Heb. 1 : 3.

The Lord our God, he it is that brought us up, and our fathers, out of the land of Egypt, from the house of bondage, and which did those great signs in our sight, and preserved us in all the way wherein we went, and among all the people through whom we passed. *Joshua* 24 : 17. O Lord, thou preservest man and beast. *Psa.* 36 : 6. The Lord upholdeth the righteous. *Psa.* 37 : 17. In him we live, and move, and have our being. *Acts* 17 : 28. By him all things consist. *Col.* 1 : 17. He that holdeth the seven stars in his right hand. *Rev.* 2 : 1.

§ 2.—MAN.

21. *Of what did God make man's body?*

Of the dust of the ground.—Gen. 2 : 7.

In the sweat of thy face shalt thou eat bread, till thou return unto the ground; for out of it wast thou taken: for dust thou art, and unto dust shalt thou return. *Gen.* 3 : 19. The Lord God sent him forth from the garden of Eden to till the ground from whence he was taken. *Gen.* 3 : 23. For he knoweth our frame; he remembereth that we are dust. *Psa.* 103 : 14. But now, O Lord, thou art our Father; we are the clay, and thou our potter. *Isa.* 64 : 8. The first man is of the earth, earthy. 1 *Cor.* 15 : 47.

22. *How did God make man's soul?*

God breathed into his nostrils the breath of life, and man became a living soul.—Gen. 2 : 7.

But there is a spirit in man: and the inspiration of the Almighty giveth them understanding. *Job* 32 : 8. The Spirit of God hath made me, and the breath of the Almighty hath given me life. *Job* 33 : 4. Who teacheth us more than the beasts of the earth, and maketh us wiser than the fowls of

heaven. *Job* 35 : 11. As the Lord liveth, that made us this soul. *Jer.* 38 : 16. The Lord, which stretcheth forth the heavens, and layeth the foundation of the earth, and formeth the spirit of man within him. *Zech.* 12 : 1. The first man Adam was made a living soul. 1 *Cor.* 15 : 45.

23. *How do the soul and body differ?*

The body is material and mortal, the soul is spiritual and immortal.

Then shall the dust return to the earth as it was; and the spirit shall return unto God who gave it. *Eccles.* 12 : 7. Fear not them which kill the body, but are not able to kill the soul. *Matt.* 10 : 28. A spirit hath not flesh and bones. *Luke* 24 : 39. Flesh and blood cannot inherit the kingdom of God. 1 *Cor.* 15 : 50.

24. *Was man created good?*

He was; God created man in his own image.—Gen. 1 : 27.

And God saw everything that he had made, and, behold, it was very good. *Gen.* 1 : 31. In the day that God created man, in the likeness of God made he him. *Gen.* 5 : 1. Thou hast made him a little lower than the angels, and hast crowned him with glory and honor. *Psa.* 8 : 5. God hath made man upright. *Eccles.* 7 : 29. He is the image and glory of God. 1 *Cor.* 11 : 7. Men, which are made after the similitude of God. *James* 3 : 9.

25. *In what did this image of God consist?*

In righteousness and true holiness.—Eph. 4 : 24.

And God said, Let us make man in our image, after our likeness. *Gen.* 1 : 26. And have put on the new man, which is renewed in knowledge after the image of him that created him. *Col.* 3 : 10.

(*See proofs of the Attributes of God. Questions* 8–12.)

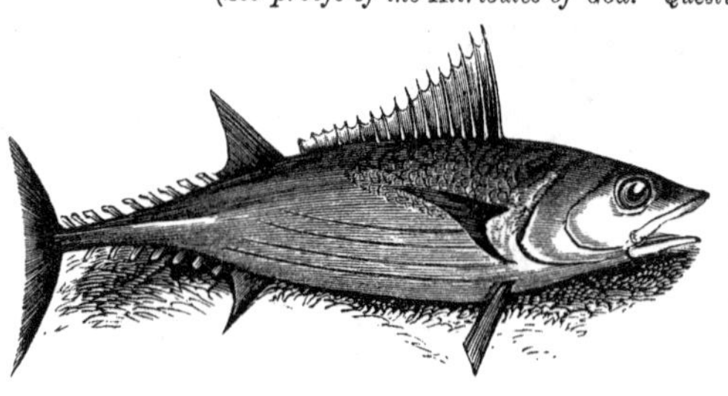

26. *What authority was given to man at the creation?*

God gave him dominion over every living thing.—Gen. 1 : 28.

Let them have dominion over the fish of the sea, and over the fowl of the air, and over the cattle, and over all the earth, and over every creeping thing that creepeth upon the earth. *Gen.* 1 : 26. Thou madest him to have dominion over the works of thy hands: thou hast put all things under his feet; all sheep and oxen, yea, and the beasts of the field; the fowl of the air, and the fish of the sea, and whatsoever passeth through the paths of the seas. *Psa.* 8 : 6–8. Thou crownedst him with glory and honor, and didst set him over the works of thy hands; thou hast put all things in subjection under his feet. *Heb.* 2 : 7, 8.

27. *Where did God place our first parents?*

In the garden of Eden.—Gen. 2 : 8.

And the Lord God planted a garden eastward in Eden; and there he put the man whom he had formed. *Gen.* 2 : 8. And the Lord God took the man, and put him into the garden of Eden, to dress it, and to keep it. *Gen.* 2 : 15.

28. *What law was given them?*

The law of perfect obedience.—Gen. 2 : 16, 17.

Of every tree of the garden thou mayest freely eat: but of the tree of the knowledge of good and evil, thou shalt not eat of it: for in the day that thou eatest thereof thou shalt surely die. *Gen.* 2 : 16, 17. By the law is the knowledge of sin. *Rom.* 3 : 20.

III. MAN'S FALL AND SINFUL STATE.

§ 1.—SIN.

29. *Did our first parents continue holy and happy?*

They sinned against God, and fell into misery.—Gen. 3.

When the woman saw that the tree was good for food, and that it was pleasant to the eyes, and a tree to be desired to make one wise, she took of the fruit thereof and did eat; and gave also unto her husband with her, and he did eat. *Gen.* 3 : 6. And the Lord God called unto Adam, and said unto him, Where art thou? And he said, I heard thy voice in the garden, and I was afraid, because I was naked; and I hid myself. *Gen.* 3 : 9, 10. By one man sin entered into the world, and death by sin. *Rom.* 5 : 12.

30. *What is sin?*

Any transgression of the law of God.—1 John 3 : 4.

By the law is the knowledge of sin. *Rom.* 3 : 20. Whosoever committeth sin transgresseth also the law; for sin is the transgression of the law. 1 *John* 3 : 4. He that committeth sin is of the devil; for the devil sinneth from the beginning. 1 *John* 3 : 8.

31. *What was the sin of our first parents?*

Their eating of the forbidden fruit.

And the Lord God commanded the man, saying, Of every tree of the garden thou mayest freely eat: but of the tree of the knowledge of good and evil, thou shalt not eat of it. *Genesis* 2 : 16, 17. She took of the fruit thereof, and did eat; and gave also unto her husband, and he did eat. *Gen.* 3 : 6.

32. *By whom were they tempted to sin?*

By the devil, in the form of a serpent.—Gen. 3 : 13; Rev. 20 : 2.

The serpent beguiled me, and I did eat. *Gen.* 3 : 13. That old serpent, called the Devil, and Satan, which deceiveth the whole world. *Rev.* 12 : 9. That old serpent, which is the Devil, and Satan. *Rev.* 20 : 2.

§ 2.—GUILT, PREVALENCE, AND CONSEQUENCES OF SIN.

33. *What evil did their sin bring upon them?*

They lost the image of God, were driven out of Eden, and became subject to pain and death.

[EXPULSION FROM PARADISE.]

Of the tree of knowledge of good and evil, thou shalt not eat of it: for in the day that thou eatest thereof, thou shalt surely die. *Gen.* 2 : 17. Cursed is the ground for thy sake; in sorrow shalt thou eat of it all the days of thy life. *Gen.* 3 : 17. Therefore the Lord God sent him forth from the garden of Eden. *Gen.* 3 : 23. So he drove out the man. *Gen.* 3 : 24. By one man sin entered into the world, and death by sin; and so death passed upon all men. *Rom.* 5 : 12. The wages of sin is death. *Rom.* 6 : 23.

34. *Did their sin harm any besides themselves?*

By the offense of one, judgment came upon all men to condemnation.—Rom. 5 : 18.

By one man sin entered into the world, and death by sin; and so death passed upon all men, for that all have sinned. *Rom.* 5 : 12. By one man's disobedience many were made sinners. *Rom.* 5 : 19.

35. *In what state are mankind born?*

In the image of fallen Adam, destitute of original righteousness.—Gen. 5 : 3.

[CAIN AND ABEL.]

Adam lived a hundred and thirty years, and begat a son in his own likeness, after his image. *Gen.* 5 : 3. God saw that the wickedness of man was great in the earth, and that every imagination of the thoughts of his heart was only evil continually. *Gen.* 6 : 5. For the imagination of man's heart is evil from his youth. *Gen.* 8 : 21. The heart is deceitful above all things, and desperately wicked. *Jer.* 17 : 9. For from within, out of the heart of men, proceed evil thoughts, adulteries, fornications, murders, thefts, covetousness, wickedness, deceit, lasciviousness, an evil eye, blasphemy, pride, foolishness. *Mark* 7 : 21, 22. There is none righteous, no, not one. *Rom.* 3 : 10.

36. *What are the miseries of this condition?*

All mankind being born in sin, are by nature under the wrath of God.

They that plow iniquity and sow wickedness, reap the same. *Job* 4 : 8. Many sorrows shall be to the wicked. *Psa.* 32 : 10. Thy way and thy doings have procured these things unto thee. *Jer.* 4 : 18. Your iniquities have turned away these things, and your sins have withholden good things from you. *Jer.* 5 : 25. Our fathers have sinned, and are not; and we have borne their iniquities. *Lam.* 5 : 7. The wages of sin is death. *Rom.* 6 : 23. And were by nature the children of wrath, even as others. *Eph.* 2 : 3. The whole world lieth in wickedness. 1 *John* 5 : 19.

IV. SALVATION.

§ 1.—THE SOURCE AND GROUNDS OF SALVATION, VIZ.: THE LOVE OF GOD IN CHRIST, AND REDEMPTION THROUGH CHRIST.

37. *Did God leave mankind in sin and misery?*

No; God so loved the world, that he gave his only-begotten Son, that whosoever believeth in him should not perish, but have everlasting life.—John 3 : 16.

This is the will of him that sent me, that every one which seeth the Son, and believeth on him, may have everlasting life. *John* 6 : 40. He that believeth on me hath everlasting life. *John* 6 : 47. In this was manifested the love of God toward us, because that God sent his only-begotten Son into the world, that we might live through him. 1 *John* 4 : 9. We have seen, and do testify, that the Father sent the Son to be the Saviour of the world. 1 *John* 4 : 14.

38. *What did the Son of God do to save sinners?*

He became man, lived, suffered, died, and rose again.

The Word was made flesh, and dwelt among us. *John* 1 : 14. It is written of the Son of man, that he must suffer many things. *Mark* 9 : 12. A

[THE BURIAL OF JESUS.]

man of sorrows, and acquainted with grief. *Isa.* 53 : 3. Christ died for our sins according to the Scriptures; and he was buried, and he rose again the third day. 1 *Cor.* 15 : 3, 4.

39. *How did he become man?*

Christ, though God, took upon him the form of a servant, and was made in the likeness of man, having a human body and soul.

But made himself of no reputation, and took upon him the form of a servant, and was made in the likeness of men. *Phil.* 2 : 7. Sacrifice and offering thou wouldest not, but a body hast thou prepared me. *Heb.* 10 : 5. My soul is exceeding sorrowful, even unto death. *Matt.* 26 : 38.

40. *What example does Christ's life afford us?*

An example of perfect goodness and holiness.

[CHRIST GIVING SIGHT TO THE BLIND.]

He had done no violence, neither was any deceit in his mouth. *Isaiah* 53 : 9. I have sinned, in that I have betrayed the innocent blood. *Matt.* 27 : 4. Have thou nothing to do with that just man. *Matt.* 27 : 19. Saying, Father, if thou be willing, remove this cup from me: nevertheless, not my will, but thine, be done. *Luke* 22 : 42. Father, forgive them. *Luke* 23 : 34. Pilate saith unto them, Take ye him, and crucify him: for I find no fault in him. *John* 19 : 6. Who went about doing good. *Acts* 10 : 38. For such a high-priest became us, who is holy, harmless, undefiled, separate from sinners. *Heb.* 7 : 26. Leaving us an example, that ye should follow his steps: who did no sin, neither was guile found in his mouth: who, when he was reviled, reviled not again; when he suffered, he threatened not. 1 *Pet.* 2 : 21–23.

41. *What did Christ suffer for us?*

He humbled himself, and became obedient unto death, even the death of the cross.—Phil. 2 : 8.

A man of sorrows, and acquainted with grief. *Isa.* 53 : 3. He hath poured out his soul unto death: and he was numbered with the trangressors. *Isa.* 53 : 12. My soul is exceeding sorrowful, even unto death. *Matt.* 26 : 38. Now is my soul troubled, and what shall I say? Father, save me from this hour: but for this cause came I unto this hour. *John* 12 : 27. Christ hath redeemed us from the curse of the law, being made a curse for us. *Gal.* 3 : 13. But made himself of no reputation, and took upon him the form of a servant. *Phil.* 2 : 7. Looking unto Jesus, the author and finisher of our faith; who, for the joy that was set before him, endured the cross, despising the shame. *Heb.* 12 : 2.

42. *Why did Christ thus suffer and die?*

To offer to divine justice full atonement for the sins of the world.

Ought not Christ to have suffered these things, and to enter into his glory? *Luke* 24 : 26. Thus it behooved Christ to suffer. *Luke* 24 : 46. Opening and alleging, that Christ must needs have suffered. *Acts* 17 : 3. When we were yet without strength, in due time Christ died for the ungodly. *Rom.* 5 : 6. While we were yet sinners, Christ died for us. *Rom.* 5 : 8. We were reconciled to God by the death of his Son. *Rom.* 5 : 10. He that spared not his own Son, but delivered him up for us all, how shall he not with him also freely give us all things? *Rom.* 8 : 32. Christ hath redeemed us from the curse of the law. *Gal.* 3 : 13. Ye who sometime were far off, are made nigh by the blood of Christ. *Eph.* 2 : 13. Christ also hath loved us, and hath given himself for us, an offering and a sacrifice to God for a sweet-smelling savor. *Eph.* 5 : 2. It is of necessity that this man have somewhat to offer. *Heb.* 8 : 3. By his own blood, he entered in once into the holy place, having obtained eternal redemption for us. *Heb.* 9 : 12. Christ, who through the eternal Spirit offered himself without spot to God. *Heb.* 9 : 14. Without shedding of blood is no remission. *Heb.* 9 : 22. It was therefore necessary that the patterns of things in the heavens should be purified with these. *Heb.* 9 : 23. Who his own self bare our sins in his own body on the tree, that we, being dead to sins, should live unto righteousness: by whose stripes ye were healed. 1 *Pet.* 2 : 24. He is the propitiation for our sins; and not for ours only, but also for the sins of the whole world. 1 *John* 2 : 2.

43. *How are we benefited by Christ's resurrection?*

He rose for our justification, and ascended to the right hand of God, where he ever liveth to make intercession for us.—Rom. 4 : 25; Eph. 1 : 20; Col. 3 : 1; Heb. 7 : 25.

[THE ASCENSION.]

Him hath God exalted with his right hand to be a Prince and a Saviour, for to give repentance to Israel and forgiveness of sins. *Acts* 5 : 31. We believe on him that raised up Jesus our Lord from the dead; who was delivered for our offenses, and was raised again for our justification. *Rom.* 4 : 24, 25. It is Christ that died, yea rather, that is risen again, who is even at the right hand of God, who also maketh intercession for us. *Rom.* 8 : 34. We have a great high-priest that is passed into the heavens, Jesus the Son of God. *Heb.* 4 : 14. But this man, because he continueth ever, hath an unchangeable priesthood. *Hebrews* 7 : 24. Christ is not entered into the holy places made with hands, which are the figures of the true; but into heaven itself, now to appear in the presence of God for us. *Hebrews* 9 : 24. If any man sin, we have an advocate with the Father, Jesus Christ the righteous. 1 *John* 2 : 1.

44. *Did Christ make this atonement for all mankind?*

By the grace of God he tasted death for every man.—Heb. 2 : 9.

God so loved the world that he gave his only-begotten Son, that whosoever believeth in him should not perish, but have everlasting life. For God sent not his Son into the world to condemn the world, but that the world through him might be saved. *John* 3 : 16, 17. He died for all. 2 *Cor.* 5 : 15. Who gave himself a ransom for all. 1 *Tim.* 2 : 6. But we see Jesus, who was made a little lower than the angels for the suffering of death, crowned with glory and honor; that he by the grace of God should taste death for every man. *Heb.* 2 : 9. And he is the propitiation for our sins: and not for ours only, but also for the sins of the whole world. 1 *John* 2 : 2.

§ 2.—CONDITIONS OF SALVATION.

45. *Will all men therefore be saved?*

No; the wicked shall be turned into hell, and all the nations that forget God.—Psa. 9 : 17.

Except ye repent, ye shall all likewise perish. *Luke* 13 : 3. And whosoever was not found written in the book of life was cast into the lake of fire. *Rev.* 20 : 15. Depart from me, all ye workers of iniquity. There shall be weeping and gnashing of teeth, when ye shall see Abraham, and Isaac, and Jacob, and all the prophets, in the kingdom of God, and you yourselves thrust out. *Luke* 13 : 27, 28. Except your righteousness shall exceed the righteousness of the scribes and Pharisees, ye shall in no case enter into the kingdom of heaven. *Matt.* 5 : 20. Taking vengeance on them that know not God, and that obey not the gospel of our Lord Jesus Christ. 2 *Thess.* 1 : 8. I will cut off the remnant of Baal . . . . and them that are turned back from the Lord; and those that have not sought the Lord, nor inquired for him. *Zeph.* 1 : 4, 6.

46. *Will those be saved who die in childhood, before they know good and evil?*

They will; for Jesus said, "Of such is the kingdom of heaven."—Matt. 19 : 14.

And they brought young children to him, that he should touch them: and his disciples rebuked those that brought them. But when Jesus saw it, he was much displeased, and said unto them, Suffer the little children to come unto me, and forbid them not: for of such is the kingdom of God. Verily I say unto you, Whosoever shall not receive the kingdom of God as a little child, he shall not enter therein. And he took them up in his arms, put his hands upon them, and blessed them. *Mark* 10 : 13–16.

[CHRIST RECEIVING CHILDREN.]

47. *On what terms are those saved who know good from evil?*

On condition of repentance toward God, and faith toward our Lord Jesus Christ.—Acts 20 : 21.

And the times of this ignorance God winked at; but now commandeth all men everywhere to repent. *Acts* 17 : 30. Repent ye therefore, and be converted, that your sins may be blotted out. *Acts* 3 : 19. Repent therefore of this thy wickedness, and pray God, if perhaps the thought of thy heart may be forgiven thee. *Acts* 8 : 22. By grace are ye saved, through faith. *Eph.* 2 : 8.

48. *What is repentance?*

A godly sorrow on account of sin.—2 Cor. 7 : 10.

For I will declare mine iniquity; I will be sorry for my sin. *Psa.* 38 : 18. Ye were made sorry after a godly manner. 2 *Cor.* 7 : 9. For godly sorrow worketh repentance to salvation not to be repented of. 2 *Cor.* 7 : 10. All of them mourning, every one for his iniquity. *Ezek.* 7 : 16. Turn ye even to me with all your heart, and with fasting, and with weeping, and with mourning; and rend your heart, and not your garments. *Joel* 2 : 12, 13.

49. *How is true repentance indicated?*

By the forsaking of sin, and a sincere turning to God.

Amend your ways and your doings. *Jer.* 7 : 3. Return ye now every man from his evil way, and amend your doings. *Jer.* 35 : 15. Let the wicked forsake his way, and the unrighteous man his thoughts: and let him return unto the Lord. *Isa.* 55 : 7. Cease to do evil; learn to do well. *Isa.* 1 : 16, 17.

50. *What is faith in Jesus Christ?*

Faith in Jesus Christ is the act of receiving, and trusting in him alone for salvation.—John 1 : 12; Phil. 3 : 9.

As many as received him, to them gave he power to become the sons of God, even to them that believe on his name. *John* 1 : 12. And be found in him, not having mine own righteousness, which is of the law, but that which is through the faith of Christ, the righteousness which is of God by faith. *Phil.* 3 : 9. Faith is the substance of things hoped for, the evidence of things not seen. *Heb.* 11 : 1.

[CHRISTIAN INSTRUCTION.]

51. *Can we repent and believe of ourselves?*

No; the power to repent and believe is given us of God.—[Eph. 2 : 8; Rom. 11 : 29.

God, having raised up his Son Jesus, sent him to bless you, in turning away every one of you from his iniquities. *Acts* 3 : 26. Him hath God exalted with his right hand to be a Prince and a Saviour, for to give repentance to Israel. *Acts* 5 : 31. Then hath God also to the Gentiles granted repentance unto life. *Acts* 11 : 18. For by grace are ye saved through faith; and that not of yourselves: it is the gift of God. *Ephesians* 2 : 8.

52. *How can we know when we believe in Jesus Christ?*

He that believeth on the Son of God hath the witness in himself.—1 John 5 : 10.

For as many as are led by the Spirit of God, they are the sons of God. *Rom.* 8 : 14. Know ye not that ye are the temple of God, and that the Spirit of God dwelleth in you? 1 *Cor.* 3 : 16. God who hath also sealed us, and given the earnest of the Spirit in our hearts. 2 *Cor.* 1 : 22.

53. *What witness is this?*

The Spirit itself beareth witness with our spirit, that we are the children of God.—Rom. 8 : 16.

Hereby know we that we dwell in him, and he in us, because he hath given us of his Spirit. 1 *John* 4 : 13. And God, which knoweth the hearts, bare them witness, giving them the Holy Ghost. *Acts* 15 : 8. Hereby we know that he abideth in us, by the Spirit which he hath given us. 1 *John* 3 : 24. And because ye are sons, God hath sent forth the Spirit of his Son into your hearts, crying, Abba, Father. *Gal.* 4 : 6.

§ 3.—THE FRUITS AND EXTENT OF SALVATION.

54. *What fruits doth this faith produce?*

Justification, regeneration, sanctification.—Rom. 5 : 1; John 1 : 12, 13; Gal. 2 : 16; 2 Thess. 2 : 13.

Therefore, being justified by faith, we have peace with God, through our Lord Jesus Christ. *Rom.* 5 : 1. Knowing that a man is not justified by the works of the law, but by the faith of Jesus Christ, even we have believed in Jesus Christ, that we might be justified by the faith of Christ. *Gal.* 2 : 16. God hath from the beginning chosen you to salvation, through sanctification of the Spirit, and belief of the truth. 2 *Thess.* 2 : 13. This is the will of God, even your sanctification. 1 *Thess.* 4 : 3.

55. *What is justification?*

Justification is that act of God's free grace in which he

pardons our sins and accepts us as righteous in his sight for the sake of Christ.—Eph. 1 : 7; 2 Cor. 5 : 21; Rom. 3 : 24; 5 : 19.

Being justified freely by his grace, through the redemption that is in Christ Jesus. *Rom.* 3 : 24. In whom we have redemption through his blood, the forgiveness of sins, according to the riches of his grace. *Eph.* 1 : 7. For he hath made him to be sin for us, who knew no sin; that we might be made the righteousness of God in him. 2 *Cor.* 5 : 21. For as by one man's disobedience many were made sinners, so by the obedience of one shall many be made righteous. *Rom.* 5 : 19.

56. *What is regeneration?*

It is the new birth of the soul in the image of Christ, whereby we become the children of God.—Eph. 1 : 5; John 1 : 12, 13; John 3 : 3; Eph. 4 : 24; 1 John 3 : 2.

Therefore if any man be in Christ, he is a new creature: old things are passed away; behold, all things have become new. 2 *Cor.* 5 : 17. That ye put on the new man, which after God is created in righteousness and true holiness. *Eph.* 4 : 24. As many as received him, to them gave he power to become the sons of God, even to them that believe on his name. *John* 1 : 12.

57. *What is sanctification?*

Sanctification is that act of divine grace whereby we are made holy.—1 Thess. 5 : 23; Eph. 1 : 4; Col. 1 : 22; Heb. 13 : 12.

Wherefore Jesus also, that he might sanctify the people with his own blood, suffered without the gate. *Heb.* 13 : 12. In the body of his flesh through death, to present you holy, and unblamable, and unreprovable in his sight. *Col.* 1 : 22. According as he hath chosen us in him before the foundation of the world, that we should be holy and without blame before him in love. *Eph.* 1 : 4. And the very God of

[THE CRUCIFIXION.]

peace sanctify you wholly; and I pray God your whole spirit, and soul, and body, be preserved blameless unto the coming of our Lord Jesus Christ. 1 *Thess.* 5 : 23.

58. *May every believer be wholly sanctified in this life?*

Yes; God's command is, Be ye holy, for I am holy; and his promise is, that if we confess our sins he will cleanse us from all unrighteousness.—1 Peter 1 : 16; 1 Thess. 4 : 3; 1 John 1 : 9.

For this is the will of God, even your sanctification. 1 *Thess.* 4 : 3. Christ loved the Church, and gave himself for it; that he might sanctify and cleanse it with the washing of water by the word, that he might present it to himself a glorious Church, not having spot, or wrinkle, or any such thing; but that it should be holy, and without blemish. *Eph.* 5 : 25–27. The blood of Jesus Christ his Son cleanseth us from all sin. 1 *John* 1 : 7. Then will I sprinkle clean water upon you, and ye shall be clean; from all your filthiness, and from all your idols, will I cleanse you. *Ezek.* 36 : 25.

59. *What is implied in being a perfect Christian, or in being wholly sanctified?*

Loving God with all our heart and soul, mind and strength, and our neighbor as ourselves.

Thou shalt love the Lord thy God with all thy heart, and with all thy soul, and with all thy mind. This is the first and great commandment. And the second is like unto it, Thou shalt love thy neighbor as thyself. On these two commandments hang all the law and the prophets. *Matt.* 22 : 37–40.

60. *Is it possible for a justified or a sanctified Christian to fall from grace and perish?*

It is; for even the apostle Paul feared lest, after having preached to others, he himself should be a castaway.—[1 Cor. 9 : 27.

Holding faith, and a good conscience; which some having put away, concerning faith have made shipwreck. 1 *Tim.* 1 : 19. For if we sin wilfully after that we have received the knowledge of the truth, there remaineth no more sacrifice for sins, but a certain fearful looking for of judgment and fiery indignation. *Heb.* 10 : 26, 27. The Lord is with you, while ye be with him; . . . but if ye forsake him, he will forsake you. 2 *Chron.* 15 : 2. But if any man draw back, my soul shall have no pleasure in him. *Heb.* 10 : 38.

61. *How shall we guard against the danger of falling from grace?*

[SECRET PRAYER.]

By watchfulness, prayer, and a life of faith in the Son of God.

Pray that ye enter not into temptation. *Luke* 22 : 40. Take ye heed, watch and pray. *Mark* 13 : 33. Wherefore, let him that thinketh he standeth, take heed lest he fall. 1 *Cor.* 10 : 12. Watch thou in all things. 2 *Tim.* 4 : 5. Pray without ceasing. 1 *Thess.* 5 : 17. Watch unto prayer. 1 *Pet.* 4 : 7.

V. THE MEANS OF GRACE.

§1.—THE CHURCH AND MINISTRY.

62. *What are the principal means of grace?*

The Church, the sacraments, the word of God, and prayer.

63. *In what two forms does the Church of God exist?*

The visible and the invisible.

64. *What is the visible Church?*

The visible Church of Christ is a congregation of faithful men, in which the pure word of God is preached and the sacraments duly administered according to Christ's ordinance.—Acts 2:42; Matt. 16:18; Eph. 5:27.

And he gave some, apostles; and some, prophets; and some, evangelists; and some, pastors and teachers; for the perfecting of the saints, for the work of the ministry, for the edifying of the body of Christ. *Eph.* 4 : 11, 12. And gave him to be the head over all things to the Church, which is his body. *Eph.* 1 : 22, 23. Then they that gladly received his word were baptized: and the same day there were added unto them about three thousand souls. And they continued steadfastly in the apostles' doctrine and fellowship, and in breaking of bread, and in prayers. *Acts* 2 : 41, 42.

65. *What is the invisible Church?*

The whole body of God's true people in every period of time.

So we, being many, are one body in Christ, and every one members one of another. *Rom.* 12 : 5. And gave him to be the head over all things to the Church, which is his body. *Eph.* 1 : 22, 23. And other sheep I have, which are not of this fold. *John* 10 : 16. But ye are come unto Mount Sion, and unto the city of the living God, the heavenly Jerusalem, and to an innumerable company of angels, to the general assembly and Church of the first-born, which are written in heaven, and to God the Judge of all, and to the spirits of just men made perfect. *Heb.* 12 : 22, 23.

66. *Ought not all persons, where the gospel is preached, to become believers in Christ and members of the Church?*

They ought; in order to have a visible union with Christ, the Head of the Church, and communion with his people.—Eph. 5 : 23; John 17 : 21; 1 Cor. 12 : 20.

That they all may be one; as thou, Father, art in me, and I in thee, that they also may be one in us. *John* 17 : 21.

67. *Who are to preach the word of God and administer the sacraments?*

Faithful men, called of God and set apart by the Church to the office and work of the ministry.—Heb. 5 : 4; Acts 13 : 2, 3; 1 Tim. 4 : 14.

And no man taketh this honor unto himself, but he that is called of God, as was Aaron. *Heb.* 5 : 4. Our sufficiency is of God; who also hath made us able ministers of the new testament; not of the letter, but of the spirit. 2 *Cor.* 3 : 5, 6. Whereof I was made a minister according to the gift of the grace of God given unto me by the effectual working of his power. *Eph.*

[PAUL PREACHING AT ATHENS.]

3 : 7. Paul, a servant of Jesus Christ, called to be an apostle, separated unto the gospel of God. *Rom.* 1 : 1. But as we were allowed of God to be put in trust with the gospel, even so we speak; not as pleasing men, but God, which trieth our hearts. 1 *Thess.* 2 : 4. For though I should boast somewhat more of our authority, (which the Lord hath given us for edification, and not for your destruction,) I should not be ashamed. 2 *Cor.* 10 : 8. As they ministered to the Lord, and fasted, the Holy Ghost said, Separate me Barnabas and Saul, for the work whereunto I have called them. And when they had fasted and prayed, and laid their hands on them, they sent them away. *Acts* 13 : 2, 3.

§ 2.—THE SACRAMENTS.

68. *How many sacraments has Christ ordained in his Church?*

Two; baptism and the Lord's supper.—Matt. 28 : 19; 1 Cor. 11 : 23–26.

And he said unto them, Go ye into all the world, and preach the gospel to every creature. He that believeth, and is baptized, shall be saved. *Mark* 16 : 15, 16. Jesus took bread, and blessed, and brake it, and gave to them, and said, Take, eat: this is my body. And he took the cup, and when he had given thanks, he gave it to them: and they all drank of it. And he said unto them, This is my blood of the new testament, which is shed for many. *Mark* 14 : 22–24.

69. *What is a sacrament?*

An outward and visible sign of an inward and spiritual grace.

(1.) BAPTISM.

70. *What is the outward sign in baptism?*

Water, applied in the name of the Father, and of the Son, and of the Holy Ghost.—John 3 : 5; Matt. 28 : 19.

See, here is water; what doth hinder me to be baptized? *Acts* 8 : 36. Can any man forbid water, that these should not be baptized? *Acts* 10 : 47. Go ye therefore, and teach all nations, baptizing them in the name of the Father, and of the Son, and of the Holy Ghost. *Matt.* 28 : 19.

71. *What is the inward grace signified in baptism?*

A death unto sin and a new birth unto righteousness.

Arise and be baptized, and wash away thy sins, calling on the name of the Lord. *Acts* 22 : 16. The like figure whereunto, even baptism, doth also now save us, (not the putting away of the filth of the flesh, but the answer of a good conscience toward God,) by the resurrection of Jesus Christ. 1 *Pet.* 3 : 21. As many of you as have been baptized into Christ have put on Christ. *Gal.* 3 : 27.

72. *What advantages are secured to baptized persons?*

They are admitted to the visible Church of Christ; their relation to him as the Mediator of the new covenant, and their title to the spiritual blessings thereto belonging, are solemnly confirmed.

I will establish my covenant between me and thee, and thy seed after thee, in their generations, for an everlasting covenant; to be a God unto thee, and to thy seed after thee. *Gen.* 17 : 7. He that believeth and is baptized, shall be saved. *Mark* 16 : 16. Repent, and be baptized every one of you in the name of Jesus Christ, for the remission of sins, and ye shall receive the gift of the Holy Ghost. *Acts* 2 : 38.

(2.) THE LORD'S SUPPER.

73. *Why was the sacrament of the Lord's supper ordained?*

For the continual remembrance of the sacrifice of Christ's death, and of the benefits that we thereby receive.—1 Cor. 11: 23–26.

Christ our passover is sacrificed for us: therefore let us keep the feast. 1 *Cor.* 5 : 7, 8. This do in remembrance of me. *Luke* 22 : 19. For as often as ye eat this bread, and drink this cup, ye do show the Lord's death till he come. 1 *Cor.* 11 : 26.

74. *What is the outward sign of the Lord's supper?*

Bread and wine, received according to Christ's command.

The Lord Jesus, the same night in which he was betrayed, took bread; and when he had given thanks, he brake it, and said, Take, eat; this is my body, which is broken for you . . . . . . after the same manner also he took the cup, when he had supped, saying, This cup is the new testament in my blood. 1 *Cor.* 11 : 23–25.

75. *What is the inward grace of this sacrament?*

The communion of the body and blood of Christ, whereby we are reminded of his sacrificial death, and spiritually strengthened to do HIS will.

The cup of blessing which we bless, is it not the communion of the blood of Christ? the bread which we break, is it not the communion of the body of Christ? 1 *Cor.* 10 : 16. Christ our passover is sacrificed for us. 1 *Cor.* 5 : 7. For as often as ye eat this bread and drink this cup, ye do show the Lord's death till he come. 1 *Cor.* 11 : 26. This do in remembrance of me. 1 *Cor.* 11 : 24. Let us have grace, whereby we may serve God acceptably, with reverence and godly fear. *Heb.* 12 : 28.

§ 3.—THE WORD OF GOD AND PRAYER.

76. *Whence do we derive all correct knowledge of religious truth and duty?*

From the Holy Bible.

77. *What is the Bible?*

It is the revelation of divine truth, and the record of God's will.

78. *What is the only sufficient rule of a Christian's faith and practice?*

The word of God, as contained in the Scriptures of the Old and New Testaments.

The law of the Lord is perfect, converting the soul; the testimony of the Lord is sure, making wise the simple. *Psa.* 19 : 7. Thou hast known the Holy Scriptures, which are able to make thee wise unto salvation through faith which is in Christ Jesus. 2 *Tim.* 3 : 15. But whoso looketh into the perfect law of liberty, and continueth therein, he being not a forgetful hearer, but a doer of the work, this man shall be blessed in his deed. *James* 1 : 25. Though we, or an angel from heaven, preach any other gospel unto you than that which we have preached unto you, let him be accursed. *Gal.* 1 : 8. For I testify unto every man that heareth the

[YOUNG TIMOTHY.]

words of the prophecy of this book, If any man shall add unto these things, God shall add unto him the plagues that are written in this book. *Revelation* 22 : 18.

79. *How should we use the Scriptures?*

We should seriously and diligently study God's holy word with prayer, that we may understand, believe, and practice the same.—John 5 : 39.

Search the Scriptures: for in them ye think ye have eternal life; and they are they which testify of me. *John* 5 : 39. Seek ye out of the book of the Lord, and read. *Isa.* 34 : 16. To the law and to the testimony. *Isa.* 8 : 20. Faith cometh by hearing, and hearing by the word of God. *Rom.* 10 : 17. But be ye doers of the word, and not hearers only. *James* 1 : 22. Open thou mine eyes, that I may behold wondrous things out of thy law. *Psa.* 119 : 18. These were more noble than those in Thessalonica, in that they received the word with all readiness of mind, and *searched* the *Scriptures daily*, whether those things were so. *Acts* 17 : 11.

80. *What is prayer?*

Prayer is the offering up of our desires unto God in the name of Christ.

Trust in him at all times; ye people, pour out your heart before him: God is a refuge for us. *Psa.* 62 : 8. Whatsoever ye shall ask the Father in my name, he will give it you. *John* 16 : 23. Let us lift up our heart with our hands unto God in the heavens. *Lam.* 3 : 41.

81. *With what should prayer be always accompanied?*

With humble confession of sin, with hearty thanksgiving for God's mercies, and sincere faith in his promises.

And I prayed unto the Lord my God, and made my confession. *Dan.* 9 : 4. Continue in prayer, and watch in the same with thanksgiving. *Col.* 4 : 2. By prayer and supplication, with thanksgiving, let your requests be made known unto God. *Phil.* 4 : 6. If any of you lack wisdom, let him ask of God . . . . But let him ask in faith, nothing wavering. *James* 1 : 5, 6. If we ask anything according to his will, he heareth us. And if we know that he hear us, whatsoever we ask, we know that we have the petitions that we desired of him. 1 *John* 5 : 14, 15.

82. *Where should we offer up our prayers?*

Publicly in the house of God, and privately in our families and in our closets.

[FAMILY WORSHIP.]

Enter into his gates with thanksgiving, and into his courts with praise: be thankful unto him, and bless his name. *Psa.* 100 : 4. If two of you shall agree on earth as touching anything that they shall ask, it shall be done for them of my Father which is in heaven. For where two or three are gathered together in my name, there am I in the midst of them. *Matt.* 18 : 19, 20. Pour out thy fury upon the families that call not on thy name. *Jer.* 10 : 25. When thou prayest, enter into thy closet; and when thou hast shut thy door, pray to thy Father which is in secret. *Matt.* 6 : 6.

83. *What special example of prayer is given us in Scripture?*

The Lord's prayer.

After this manner therefore pray ye. *Matt.* 6 : 9.

84. *Can you repeat the Lord's prayer?*

Our Father which art in heaven, hallowed be thy name.

Thy kingdom come. Thy will be done in earth as it is in heaven. Give us this day our daily bread. And forgive us our trespasses, as we forgive them that trespass against us. And lead us not into temptation, but deliver us from evil. For thine is the kingdom, and the power, and the glory, forever. Amen.

VI. GOD'S LAW.

DUTIES TO GOD AND MAN.

85. *What does God require of man?*

Obedience to his revealed will.

Fear God, and keep his commandments: for this is the whole duty of man. *Eccles.* 12 : 13. What doth the Lord thy God require of thee, but to fear the Lord thy God, to walk in all his ways . . . . and to serve the Lord thy God with all thy heart, and with all thy soul. *Deut.* 10 : 12.

86. *What is the rule of our obedience?*

The moral law.

If thou wilt enter into life, keep the commandments. *Matt.* 19 : 17.

87. *Where is the moral law given?*

In the ten commandments.—Exod. 20 : 1-17.

88. *What is the first commandment?*

Thou shalt have no other gods before me.

Thou shalt worship the Lord thy God, and him only shalt thou serve. *Matt.* 4 : 10. Take ye therefore good heed unto yourselves . . . . lest thou lift up thine eyes unto heaven, and when thou seest the sun, and the moon, and the stars, even all the host of heaven, shouldest be driven to worship them, and serve them. *Deut.* 4 : 15, 19. I am the Lord thy God from the land of Egypt, and thou shalt know no God but me. *Hosea* 13 : 4.

[A HINDOO IDOL.]

89. *What is the second commandment?*

Thou shalt not make unto thee any graven image, or any likeness of anything that is in heaven above, or that is in the earth beneath, or that is in the water under the earth: thou shalt not bow down thyself to them, nor serve them: for I the Lord thy God am a jealous God, visiting the iniquity of the fathers upon the children unto the third and fourth generation of them that hate me; and showing mercy unto thousands of them that love me, and keep my commandments.

Take ye therefore good heed unto yourselves . . . . lest ye corrupt yourselves, and make you a graven image, the similitude of any figure. *Deut.* 4 : 15, 16. Thou shalt worship no other god: for the Lord, whose name is Jealous, is a jealous God. *Exod.* 34 : 14.

90. *What is the third commandment?*

Thou shalt not take the name of the Lord thy God in vain: for the Lord will not hold him guiltless that taketh his name in vain.

I say unto you, Swear not at all: neither by heaven; for it is God's throne: nor by the earth; for it is his footstool: neither by Jerusalem; for it is the city of the great King: neither shalt thou swear by thy head; because thou canst not make one hair white or black. But let your communication be, Yea, yea; Nay, nay: for whatsoever is more than these cometh of evil. *Matt.* 5 : 34–37.

91. *What is the fourth commandment?*

Remember the Sabbath-day, to keep it holy. Six days shalt thou labor, and do all thy work: but the seventh day is the Sabbath of the Lord thy God: in it thou shalt not do any work, thou, nor thy son, nor thy daughter, thy man-servant, nor thy maid-servant, nor thy cattle, nor thy stranger that is within thy gates: for in six days the Lord made heaven and earth, the sea and all that in them is, and rested the seventh day: wherefore the Lord blessed the Sabbath-day, and hallowed it.

Ye shall keep my Sabbaths, and reverence my sanctuary: I am the Lord. *Lev.* 19 : 30. Six days shall work be done: but the seventh day is the Sabbath of rest, a holy convocation; ye shall do no work therein. *Lev.* 23 : 3. It is a sign between me and the children of Israel forever: for in six days the Lord made heaven and earth, and on the seventh day he rested, and was refreshed. *Exod.* 31 : 17. God blessed the seventh day, and sanctified it. *Gen.* 2 : 3. Six days thou shalt do thy work, and on the seventh day thou shalt rest. *Exod.* 23 : 12. If thou turn away thy foot from the Sabbath, from doing thy pleasure on my holy day; and call the Sabbath a delight, the holy of the Lord, honorable; and shalt honor him, not doing thine own ways, nor finding thine own pleasure, nor speaking thine own words: then shalt thou delight thyself in the Lord; and I will cause thee to ride upon the high places of the earth, and feed thee with the heritage of Jacob thy father. *Isa.* 58 : 13, 14.

[THE SANCTUARY.]

92. *What is the fifth commandment?*

Honor thy father and thy mother; that thy days may be long upon the land which the Lord thy God giveth thee.

Honor thy father and thy mother. *Matt.* 19 : 19. Children, obey your parents in the Lord: for this is right. Honor thy father and mother, (which is the first commandment with promise,) that it may be well with thee, and thou mayest live long on the earth. *Eph.* 6 : 1–3.

93. *What is the sixth commandment?*

Thou shalt not kill.

Whosoever hateth his brother is a murderer: and ye know that no murderer hath eternal life abiding in him. 1 *John* 3 : 15.

94. *What is the seventh commandment?*

Thou shalt not commit adultery.

No unclean person . . . . hath any inheritance in the kingdom . . . . of

God. *Eph.* 5 : 5. But fornication, and all uncleanness, or covetousness, let it not be once named among you. *Eph.* 5 : 3. Whosoever looketh on a woman to lust after her, hath committed adultery with her already in his heart. *Matt.* 5 : 28.

95. *What is the eighth commandment?*

Thou shalt not steal.

Thou shalt not defraud thy neighbor, neither rob him. *Lev.* 19 : 13. Ye shall not steal, neither deal falsely. *Lev.* 19 : 11.

96. *What is the ninth commandment?*

Thou shalt not bear false witness against thy neighbor.

Speak not evil one of another. *James* 4 : 11. Let all . . . . evil-speaking be put away from you. *Eph.* 4 : 31. Thou shalt not raise a false report: put not thy hand with the wicked to be an unrighteous witness. *Exod* 23 : 1. All liars shall have their part in the lake which burneth with fire and brimstone: which is the second death. *Rev.* 21 : 8.

97. *What is the tenth commandment?*

Thou shalt not covet thy neighbor's house, thou shalt not covet thy neighbor's wife, nor his man-servant, nor his maid-servant, nor his ox, nor his ass, nor anything that is thy neighbor's.

Let your conversation be without covetousness; and be content with such things as ye have. *Heb.* 13 : 5. Covetousness, let it not be once named among you, as becometh saints. *Eph.* 5 : 3. Neither shalt thou desire . . . . anything that is thy neighbor's. *Deut.* 5 : 21. Take heed, and beware of covetousness. *Luke* 12 : 15.

98. *What is our Saviour's summary of God's commandments?*

He said: Thou shalt love the Lord thy God with all thy heart, and with all thy soul, and with all thy mind. This is the first and great commandment. And the second is like unto it, Thou shalt love thy neighbor as thyself. On these two commandments hang all the law and the prophets.—Matt. 22 : 37–40.

99. *How does our Saviour explain the commandments?*

He teaches that they not only forbid sin in act, but in thought.—Matt. 5 : 21, 22, 27, 28.

Ye have heard that it was said by them of old time, Thou shalt not commit adultery: but I say unto you, That whosoever looketh on a woman to lust after her, hath committed adultery with her already in his heart. *Matt.* 5 : 27, 28.

100. *What is our Lord's precept, commonly called the golden rule?*

Whatsoever ye would that men should do to you, do ye even so to them.—Matt. 7 : 12.

Thou shalt love thy neighbor as thyself. *Gal.* 5 : 14. Say not, I will do so to him as he hath done to me; I will render to the man according to his work. *Prov.* 24 : 29.

101. *Can any man be saved by keeping the law?*

No; by the deeds of the law shall no flesh be justified. [Rom. 3 : 20.

If thou, Lord, shouldest mark iniquities, O Lord, who shall stand? *Psa.* 130 : 3. For in thy sight shall no man living be justified. *Psa.* 143 : 2. For as many as are of the works of the law, are under the curse . . . . no man is justified by the law in the sight of God. *Gal.* 3 : 10, 11.

102. *What then is the use of the law?*

It serves to show men their need of Christ; for by the law is the knowledge of sin.—Rom. 3 : 20; Gal. 3 : 19.

The law was our schoolmaster to bring us unto Christ, that we might be justified by faith. But after that faith is come, we are no longer under a schoolmaster. *Gal.* 3 : 24, 25. The law . . . . was added because of transgressions. *Gal.* 3 : 19.

103. *Are all Christians under obligation to keep the law?*

Yes; they are not without law to God, but under the law to Christ.—1 Cor. 9 : 21.

Circumcision is nothing, and uncircumcision is nothing, but the keeping of the commandments of God. 1 *Cor.* 7 : 19. Think not that I am come to destroy the law, or the prophets: I am not come to destroy, but to fulfill. For verily I say unto you, Till heaven and earth pass, one jot or one tittle shall in no wise pass from the law, till all be fulfilled. *Matt.* 5 : 17, 18.

VII. OF DEATH, JUDGMENT, AND ETERNITY.

104. *Do we remain long in this world?*

No; life is short and uncertain, and we all must die.— [Job 14 : 10.

Man dieth, and wasteth away: yea, man giveth up the ghost. *Job* 14 : 10. Man is of few days. *Job* 14 : 1. It is appointed unto men once to die. *Heb.* 9 : 27. What man is he that liveth and shall not see death? *Psa.* 89 : 48. I know that thou wilt bring me to death, and to the house appointed for all living. *Job* 30 : 23. For the living know that they shall die. *Eccles.* 9 : 5. Whereas ye know not what shall be on the morrow. For what is your life? It is even a vapor, that appeareth for a little time, and then vanisheth away. *James* 4 : 14.

105. *Is it not a fearful thing to die?*

It is to all but true Christians.

It is a fearful thing to fall into the hands of the living God. *Heb.* 10 : 31. Blessed are the dead which die in the Lord. *Rev.* 14 : 13.

106. *Why should not true Christians fear to die?*

Because the sting of death is removed, and they know that they shall go to heaven.

"I see them walking in an air of glory."

O death, where is thy sting? O grave, where is thy victory? Thanks be to God which giveth us the victory, through our Lord Jesus Christ. 1 *Cor.* 15 : 55, 57. I will ransom them from the power of the grave; I will redeem them from death: O death, I will be thy plagues; O grave, I will be thy destruction. *Hosea* 13 : 14. The Lord of hosts . . . . will swallow up death in victory. *Isa.* 25 : 8. For we know that, if our earthly house of this tabernacle were dissolved, we have a building of God, a house not made with hands, eternal in the heavens. 2 *Cor.* 5 : 1. To an inheritance incorruptible, and undefiled, and that fadeth not away, reserved in heaven for you. 1 *Peter* 1 : 4.

107. *How long will the bodies of men lie in the grave?*

Until the last day, when Christ shall come to raise the dead for judgment.

Behold, he cometh . . . . and every eye shall see him. *Rev.* 1 : 7. The Lord Jesus Christ, who shall judge the quick and the dead at his appearing. 2 *Tim.* 4 : 1. When the Son of man shall come in his glory, and all the holy angels with him, then shall he sit upon the throne of his glory: and before him shall be gathered all nations. *Matt.* 25 : 31, 32.

108. *Will all the dead be raised?*

There shall be a resurrection of the dead, both of the just and unjust.—Acts 24 : 15; John 5 : 28, 29.

I saw the dead, small and great, stand before God. *Rev.* 20 : 12. Before him shall be gathered all nations. *Matt.* 25 : 32. All that are in the graves shall hear his voice, and shall come forth; they that have done good . . . . and they that have done evil. *John* 5 : 28, 29. In Christ shall all be made alive. 1 *Cor.* 15 : 22. The trumpet shall sound, and the dead shall be raised. 1 *Cor.* 15 : 52.

109. *Will all men be judged at the last day?*

We must all appear before the judgment seat of Christ; that *every one* may receive the things done in his body, according to that he hath done, whether it be good or bad.—2 Cor. 5 : 10.

Because he hath appointed a day in the which he will judge the world in righteousness. *Acts* 17 : 31. We shall all stand before the judgment-seat of Christ. *Rom.* 14 : 10. God shall judge the righteous and the wicked. *Eccles.* 3 : 17. The Lord shall judge the ends of the earth. 1 *Sam.* 2 : 10. And they were judged every man according to their works. *Rev.* 20 : 13. The Son of man . . . . shall reward every man according to his works. *Matt.*

16 : 27. My reward is with me, to give every man according as his work shall be. *Rev.* 22 : 12.

110. *What sentence will Christ pronounce on the wicked?*

Depart from me, ye cursed, into everlasting fire, prepared for the devil and his angels.—Matt. 25 : 41.

Depart from me, all ye workers of iniquity. *Luke* 13 : 27. The chaff he will burn with fire unquenchable. *Luke* 3 : 17. He that despised Moses's law died without mercy . . . . of how much sorer punishment, suppose ye, shall he be thought worthy, who hath trodden under foot the Son of God, and hath counted the blood of the covenant, wherewith he was sanctified, an unholy thing, and hath done despite unto the Spirit of grace? *Heb.* 10 : 28, 29.

111. *What will he say to the righteous?*

Come, ye blessed of my Father, inherit the kingdom prepared for you from the foundation of the world.—Matt. 25 : 34.

I appoint unto you a kingdom as my Father hath appointed unto me. *Luke* 22 : 29. Eye hath not seen, nor ear heard, neither have entered into the heart of man, the things which God hath prepared for them that love him. 1 *Cor.* 2 : 9.

112. *What will then take place?*

The world shall be destroyed by fire; and the wicked shall go away into everlasting punishment, but the righteous into life eternal.—Matt. 25 : 46; 2 Pet. 3 : 10.

The heavens, being on fire, shall be dissolved, and the elements shall melt with fervent heat. 2 *Pet.* 3 : 12. The earth also, and the works that are therein, shall be burned up. 2 *Pet.* 3 : 10. The heavens and the earth, which are now, by the same word are kept in store, reserved unto fire against the day of judgment and perdition of ungodly men. 2 *Pet.* 3 : 7.

Appendix.

V. BAPTISMAL COVENANT.

I RENOUNCE the devil and all his works, the vain pomp and glory of the world, with all covetous desires of the same, and the sinful desires of the flesh, so that I will not follow nor be led by them.

[THE ASCENSION.]

I believe in God the Father Almighty, Maker of heaven and earth; and in Jesus Christ his only Son our Lord; who was conceived by the Holy Ghost, born of the Virgin Mary, suffered under Pontius Pilate; was crucified, dead, and buried; the third day he rose from the dead; he ascended into heaven, and sitteth on the right hand of God the Father Almighty; from thence he shall come to judge the quick and the dead.

I believe in the Holy Ghost; the holy catholic*

* By the holy catholic Church is meant the Church of God in general.

Church; the communion of saints; the forgiveness of sins; the resurrection of the body, and the life everlasting. *Amen.*

Having been baptized in this faith, I will obediently keep God's holy will and commandments, and walk in the same all the days of my life, God being my helper.

I renounce

Have no fellowship with the unfruitful works of darkness. *Eph.* 5 : 11. See also *Prov.* 4 : 14, 15; 2 *Cor.* 6 : 14, 15.

The devil and all his works,

He that committeth sin is of the devil; for the devil sinneth from the beginning. For this purpose the Son of God was manifested, that he might destroy the works of the devil. Whosoever is born of God doth not commit sin; for his seed remaineth in him; and he cannot sin because he is born of God. In this the children of God are manifest, and the children of the devil. 1 *John* 3 : 8–10. See also *John* 8 : 44; *James* 4 : 7; *Eph.* 4 : 27.

The vain pomp and glory of the world,

Love not the world, neither the things that are in the world. If any man love the world, the love of the Father is not in him.

With all covetous desires of the same, and the sinful desires of the flesh, so that I will not follow nor be led by them.

For all that is in the world, the lust of the flesh, and the lust of the eyes, and the pride of life, is not of the Father, but is of the world. 1 *John* 2 : 15, 16. See also *Rom.* 12 : 2; *Rom.* 8 : 13; *Gal.* 5 : 24.

I believe in God the Father

To us there is but one God, the Father, of whom are all things. 1 *Cor.* 8 : 6. See *Isa.* 64 : 8; *Mal.* 2 : 10.

Almighty,

Holy, holy, holy, Lord God Almighty, which was, and is, and is to come. *Rev.* 4 : 8. See *Gen.* 17 : 1.

Maker of heaven and earth:

In the beginning God created the heaven and the earth. *Gen.* 1 : 1. See *Neh.* 9 : 6; *Acts* 4 : 24.

And in Jesus Christ

And one Lord Jesus Christ, by whom are all things, and we by him. 1 *Cor.* 8 : 6. See *Luke* 2 : 21; *John* 1 : 41; *Acts* 16 : 31.

His only Son

For God so loved the world, that he gave his only-begotten Son, that whosoever believeth in him should not perish, but have everlasting life. *John* 3 : 16. See also *Matt.* 3 : 17; *John* 1 : 18.

Our Lord;

Ye call me Master and Lord: and ye say well; for so I am. *John* 13 : 13. See also *John* 20 : 18.

Who was conceived by the Holy Ghost,

Now the birth of Jesus Christ was on this wise: When as his mother Mary was espoused to Joseph, before they came together, she was found with child of the Holy Ghost. *Matt.* 1 : 18. See also verse 20, and *Luke* 1 : 35.

Born of the Virgin Mary,

Joseph also went up from Galilee, out of the city of Nazareth, into Judea, unto the city of David, which is called Bethlehem, (because he was of the house and lineage of David,) to be taxed with Mary his espoused wife, being great with child. And so it was, that, while they were there, the days were accomplished that she should be delivered. And she brought forth her first-born Son, and wrapped him in swaddling clothes, and laid him in a manger; because there was no room for them in the inn. *Luke* 2 : 4–7. See also *Isa.* 7 : 14; *Micah* 5 : 2; *Matt.* 1 : 22, 23.

Suffered under Pontius Pilate,

And so Pilate, willing to content the people, released Barabbas unto them, and delivered Jesus, when he had scourged him, to be crucified. *Mark* 15 : 15. See *Isa.* 53 : 4, 5; *Dan.* 9 : 26; *Matt.* 27 : 1, 2, 24–32.

Was crucified,

And it was the third* hour, and they crucified him. And the superscription of his accusation was written over, The King of the Jews. And with him they crucify two thieves; the one on his right hand, and the other on his left. And the scripture was fulfilled, which saith, And he was numbered with the transgressors. *Mark* 15 : 25–28. See also *Matt.* 27 : 45, 46; *John* 3 : 14, 15; 1 *Cor.* 1 : 23; *Gal.* 6 : 14.

Dead,

But when they came to Jesus, and saw that he was dead already, they brake not his legs. *John* 19 : 33. See also *Luke* 23 : 46; *Mark* 15 : 38, 39.

And buried;

Now in the place where he was crucified there was a garden; and in the garden a new sepulcher, wherein was never man yet laid. There laid they Jesus therefore because of the Jews' preparation-day; for the sepulcher was nigh at hand. *John* 19 : 41, 42. See also *Matt.* 27 : 57–60; *Isa.* 53 : 9.

The third day he rose from the dead;

The angels said unto them, Why seek ye the living among the dead? He is not here, but

* Nine o'clock in the morning.

is risen: remember how he spake unto you, when he was yet in Galilee, saying, The Son of man must be delivered into the hands of sinful men, and be crucified, and the third day rise again. *Luke* 24 : 5–7. See also *John* 2 : 19; *Matt.* 12 : 40; 28 : 1, 2, &c.; *Acts* 2 : 24, 30; 1 *Cor.* 15 : 4, 14.

He ascended into heaven, and sitteth on the right hand of God the Father Almighty.

And when he had spoken these things, while they beheld, he was taken up; and a cloud received him out of their sight. And while they looked steadfastly toward heaven as he went up, behold, two men stood by them in white apparel; which also said, Ye men of Galilee, why stand ye gazing up into heaven? This same Jesus, which is taken up from you into heaven, shall so come in like manner as ye have seen him go into heaven. *Acts* 1 : 9–11. See also *Mark* 16 : 19; *Luke* 24 : 51; *Acts* 7 : 55, 56; *Psa.* 68 : 18; *Heb.* 10 : 12.

From thence he shall come to judge the quick and the dead.

When the Son of man shall come in his glory, and all the holy angels with him, then shall he sit upon the throne of his glory: and before him shall be gathered all nations: and he shall separate them one from another, as a shepherd divideth his sheep from the goats: and he shall set the sheep on his right hand, but the goats on the left. *Matt.* 25 : 31–33. See also *Acts* 1 : 11; 10 : 42; 2 *Tim.* 4 : 1, 8; *Job* 19 : 25; *Matt.* 16 : 27.

I believe in the Holy Ghost;

And suddenly there came a sound from heaven as of a rushing mighty wind, and it filled all the house where they were sitting. And there appeared unto them cloven tongues, like as of fire, and it sat upon each of them. And they were all filled with the Holy Ghost. *Acts* 2 : 2–4. See also 2 *Cor.* 13 : 14; *Acts* 5 : 3, 4; *John* 14 : 16, 17, 26.

The holy catholic Church; the communion of saints;

For as the body is one, and hath many members, and all the members of that one body, being many, are one body: so also is Christ. For by one Spirit are we all baptized into one body, whether we be Jews or Gentiles, whether we be bond or free; and have been all made to drink into one Spirit. 1 *Cor.* 12 : 12, 13. See also *Acts* 2 : 44–47; *Rom.* 12 : 4, 5; *Eph.* 2 : 19, 20; 5 : 23–27; 1 *Tim.* 3 : 15; *Heb.* 12 : 22, 23.

The forgiveness of sins;

If any man sin, we have an advocate with the Father, Jesus Christ the righteous: and he is the propitiation for our sins: and not for ours only, but also for the sins of the whole world. 1 *John* 2 : 1, 2. See also *Isa.* 1 : 18; *Matt.* 6 : 14, 15; *Acts* 13 : 38; *Col.* 1 : 14.

The resurrection of the body,

For since by man came death, by man came also the resurrection of the dead. For as in Adam all die, even so in Christ shall all be made alive. 1 *Cor.* 15 : 21, 22. See also *John* 5 : 28, 29; 1 *Cor.* 15 : 42–44; *Job* 19 : 26, 27.

And the life everlasting. *Amen.*

And these shall go away into everlasting punishment; but the righteous into life eternal. *Matt.* 25 : 46. See also *Isa.* 25 : 8; 1 *Cor.* 15 : 54; *Dan.* 12 : 2; *John* 10 : 27, 28.

Having been baptized in this faith, I will obediently keep God's holy will and commandments,

If ye love me, keep my commandments. *John* 14 : 15. He that loveth me not, keepeth not my sayings. *John* 14 : 24.

And walk in the same all the days of my life,

He that endureth to the end shall be saved. *Matt.* 10 : 22.

God being my helper.

Without me ye can do nothing. *John* 15 : 5. I can do all things through Christ which strengtheneth me. *Phil.* 4 : 13.

Introduction.

S intimated in the Preface, this number of the catechetical series is designed for an advanced grade of study. The aim of Nos. 1 and 2 in the series was to condense, in the briefest and simplest language, all essential Scriptural truth. The aim of No. 3 is to expand that truth into fair, if not full proportions. Its plan presupposes the thorough learning of the questions and answers of the Catechism and of the Scripture proofs sustaining the positions affirmed.

The next thing requisite is to accustom the learner to state in a summary form what he has learned on the different topics. After this, the several truths embraced in each topic should be stated separately in their proper order, that the mind of the learner may form a distinct comprehension of them and of their appropriate relations to other truths.

When students have learned first to sum up, and then to analyze, a given section, they are prepared for the additional and explanatory questions and answers.

Into these questions and answers a great number of important subjects are introduced in their appropriate connections.

Some of the questions relate to the theory, and some to the practice, of religion; some of them are found in other Catechisms, and some are new. None have been inserted for the sake of extending the work, and none that have been deemed essential to the practical objects of a Catechism have been omitted. It is hoped that they will all be systematically and thoroughly learned in their proper order. Many of them will doubtless be suggestive of other questions, which an intelligent and judicious teacher can verbally supply.

The study of this Catechism will not be completed until the learner shall have prepared himself to give concise and pertinent definitions to all the important terms used.

Definitions of the more prominent and difficult terms have been appended to the several sections. It should be observed that these definitions are not intended to supply the place of a dictionary, but simply to give a concise and clear explanation of the words as used in the positions to which reference is made. Hence there has been no attempt to reduce words to their original form; on the other hand, words of every form, whether noun, verb, participle, adjective, or adverb, are defined as they occur.

It is very important for Biblical students and teachers to accustom themselves to define words clearly and properly. Continued practice will cause the habit to become pleasant as well as useful.

The design of this Catechism, throughout, is not only to exercise the memory, but to discipline the mind, to enlighten the understanding, and to improve the heart. In its preparation, constant reference has been made to the elaborate catechetical works of former times, with the intention of copying their excellences and improving upon their construction and phraseology.

It is hoped that the study of this manual of Christian truth may become universal in our Sunday schools and in our FAMILIES, and that the day will soon come when no person among us of sufficient age will be found ignorant of its contents, or unable to give a reason of the hope that is in him.

The preliminary study of Nos. 1 and 2 will render progress in No. 3 at once easy and pleasant; while the study of No. 3 will bring out the enlarged meaning and important applications of truths, which, although previously learned, would, without this succeeding study, have remained comparatively obscure and undeveloped in the mind.

This kind of study should become habitual with Christians. As they advance in years, they should grow in knowledge as well as in grace; not so much attempting to learn new things as to "comprehend with all saints what is the breadth, and length, and depth, and height" of the truth of God, which may long have been familiar to them in its elements.

Catechism, Third Form

SUMMARY AND ANALYSIS.

I. GOD.

§ 1.—HIS NATURE AND ATTRIBUTES.—Questions 1–12.

SUMMARY.

W*HAT do you know respecting the nature and attributes of God?*

A. God is my Creator, and the Creator of all things. He is an uncreated Spirit, everywhere present, all-wise, almighty, and eternal. "God is love." God is holy, merciful, just, and true.

ANALYSIS.

Q. What doctrines are stated in the summary?

A. 1. The spirituality of God.
2. His omnipresence.
3. His wisdom.
4. His omnipotence.

5. His eternity.
6. His love.
7. His holiness.
8. His mercy.
9. His justice.
10. His truth.

Explanatory and Practical Questions.

Q. What is a spirit?

A. A thinking being without bodily substance.

Q. Can you mention some created spirits?

A. Angels, both good and bad, and the souls of men.

Q. Wherein does God's spirituality differ from that of angels and the souls of men?

A. It is self-existent.

Q. What is meant by God's eternity?

A. That he is without beginning and without end.

Q. How should we think of God?

A. With fear and love.

Q. How should we speak of God?

A. With reverence and praise.

Definitions.

Omnipotence. Possessing all power.
Omnipresence. Being in all places at once.
Holiness. Freedom from sin, and infinite purity.
Love. Tender affection.
Fear. Holy awe.
Reverence. Profound respect, devout regard.
Praise. Thanksgiving and acknowledgment of excellency.

§ 2.—PERSONS OF GOD.—Questions 13–18.

SUMMARY.

Q. What is the Scripture doctrine of the persons of God?

A. There is but one God; but there are three persons in the Godhead—the Father, the Son, and the Holy Ghost—and these are equal in power and glory. The name of the Holy Trinity is to be used in the formula of Christian baptism.

ANALYSIS.

Q. What are the doctrines of this section?

A. 1. The unity of God.

2. The trinity of persons in the unity of the Divine Being.

3. The Holy Trinity is to be recognized in the most common and important ceremonies of Christianity; *e. g.*, in the formula of baptism and of the apostolic benediction.—[Matt. xxviii, 19; 2 Cor. xiii, 14.

Explanatory and Practical Questions.

Q. To what great error of mankind does the doctrine of God's unity stand opposed?

A. To polytheism, or the worship of many gods.

[WORSHIP OF THE LAMA.]

Q. What sin is almost universal under a belief in more gods than one?

A. Idolatry, which has been practiced by all heathen nations.

Q. Should we believe the less in the doctrine of the Holy Trinity, because we cannot comprehend the triune mode of God's existence?

A. No; for many facts both in nature and in the mode of our own existence are beyond our comprehension, but not the less facts.

Q. What says the apostle Paul concerning the mystery of this subject?

A. "Without controversy, great is the mystery of godliness: God was manifest in the flesh, justified in the Spirit, seen of angels, preached unto the Gentiles, believed on in the world, received up into glory."—1 Tim. iii, 16; Eph. iii. 4; v, 32; Col. ii, 2; 1 Tim. iii, 9.

Q. What evidences have we that the Father is a distinct divine person?

A. Several; the term Father is itself a personal title, and works implying personal existence are in numerous instances ascribed to the Father in the Scriptures.

Q. What evidences have we that the Son is a distinct divine person?

A. Many; the term Son is a personal title, and to him also personal works are in numerous instances ascribed in the Scriptures.

Q. What can you say of the personality of the Holy Ghost?

A. The Holy Ghost is the third person of the Holy Trinity, equal in power and glory to the Father and the Son.

Q. What general offices are ascribed in Scripture to the Holy Ghost?

A. Works of creation and providence, and the gift of inspiration.—Gen. i, 2; Psa. civ, 30; 2 Tim. iii, 16; 2 Pet. i, 21.

Q. What offices did the Holy Ghost perform for Christ?

A. He framed the human nature of Christ, and gave to him wisdom and grace without measure.—Luke i, 35; ii, 52; Isa. lxi, 1.

Q. What offices does the Holy Ghost perform with reference to sinners?

A. He convinces them of sin, and strives with them, that they may repent and believe.

Q. What offices does the Holy Ghost perform for those who believe in Christ?

A. He enlightens their minds to understand the Scriptures; assists them in their prayers; bears witness with their spirits that they are the children of God; comforts them in trouble; sanctifies them from all sin, inward and outward; fills their hearts with perfect love to God and to all mankind, and with other excellent grace and virtues.—John xvi, 13; Rom. viii, 16, 26; John xiv, 26; Gal. v, 22, 23.

Q. What offices does the Holy Ghost perform for the Church of Christ?

A. He calls and qualifies men, from time to time, to preach the word, and minister the sacraments; renders their preaching effectual to the conversion of sinners, and the edification of believers; and is present in all the ordinances of public worship.—[Acts xx, 28; 1 Thess. i, 5; John xiv, 16.

Q. By what means may you obtain the help and comfort of the Holy Spirit?

A. By prayer.—Luke xi, 13.

Definitions.

Unity. Oneness.
Triune. Three in one.
Comprehend. Fully understand.
Idolatry. The worship of idols.
Formula. Prescribed form.
Edification. Building up.

[FIELD NEAR BETHLEHEM.]

II. CREATION.

§ 1.—THE WORLD.—Questions 19, 20.

SUMMARY.

Q. What is the doctrine of the creation as it respects the world?

A. God is the Creator and upholder of all things that exist.

Explanatory and Practical Questions.

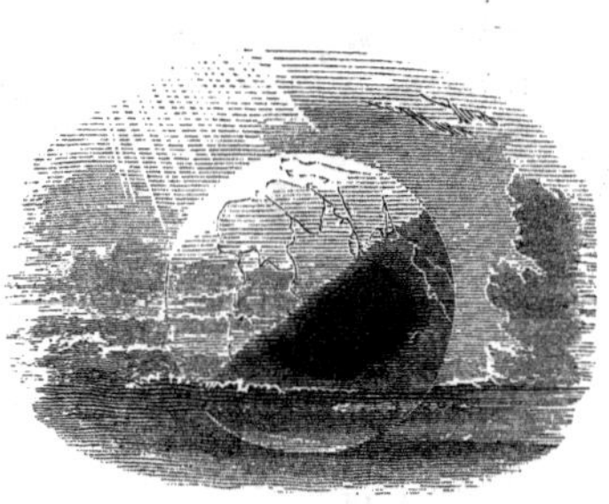

Q. What are the most prominent objects of the material creation?

A. The earth and the heavenly bodies.

Q. What objects upon the earth's surface specially display the greatness of God's creative power and wisdom?

A. Mountains, forests, continents, islands, oceans, and rivers.

Q. What smaller objects also indicate God's power and wisdom?

A. Plants, flowers, insects, fishes, birds, and animals of countless varieties; all possessing powers and qualities adapted to the elements in which they have their being, and to the end for which they were made.

Q. What great purposes are obvious throughout the creation of God?

A. The manifestation of his own glory and the happiness of his creatures.

Q. What do we understand by God's providence?

A. His most holy, wise, and powerful preservation and government of all his creatures, great and small.

Q. Ought not God's providence to be recognized in all the events and concerns of life?

A. It ought; for nothing can happen by chance. Not even a sparrow can fall on the ground without our heavenly Father.—Matt. x, 29.

Q. Is it possible for man to CREATE *anything?*

A. Not the least thing.

QUESTION FOR THOUGHT. *In which does God's glory most appear, in the greater or minuter objects of creation?*

Definitions.

Elements. The matter or substance composing the world.
Purpose. Intent, design.
Manifestation. Exhibition, display.
Happiness. Enjoyment, comfort.
Providence. Superintending care.
Preservation. Keeping in being.
Government. Rule and direction.

§ 2.—MAN.—QUESTIONS 21–28.

SUMMARY.

Q. What Scripture truths can you state respecting man?

A. God made man's body out of the dust of the ground, and breathed into his nostrils the breath of life; and man became a living soul. Man's body is material and mortal; his soul is spiritual and immortal. Man was created good and in the image of God; that is, righteous and holy. God gave man dominion over every living thing; and he dwelt in the garden of Eden, subject to the law of perfect obedience.

ANALYSIS.

Q. What doctrines are stated in this section?

A. 1. The materiality and mortality of man's body.
2. The immateriality and immortality of his soul.
3. The original righteousness of man's character.

Explanatory and Practical Questions.

Q. Is God our Creator as truly as he was the Creator of Adam?

A. He is. "It is he that hath made us, and not we ourselves."—[Psa. c, 3.

Q. Was the body of man created mortal?

A. It was not. Death is the consequence of sin.

Q. What is your soul?

A. That within me which thinks, knows, and wills, wishes and desires, rejoices and is sorry.

Q. What will become of the soul when the body is dead?

A. It will continue to exist. It cannot die like the body.

Q. Is not your soul then of great value?

A. It is of more value than the whole world.—Mark viii, 36.

Q. On what does the happiness of the soul depend?

A. On its righteousness and holiness.

Q. Whence only can we derive righteousness and holiness?

A. From God, through faith in Christ.

Definitions.

Dominion. Rule, government.
Materiality. The being composed of matter.
Mortality. Liability to die.
Immateriality. Spiritual existence, of which matter is no part.
Original. From the beginning.
The whole world. All earthly possessions.

III. MAN'S FALL AND SINFUL STATE.

§ 1.—SIN. § 2.—GUILT, PREVALENCE, AND CONSEQUENCES OF SIN.—QUESTIONS 29–36.

SUMMARY.

Q. What does the Bible teach us respecting the fall and sinful state of man?

A. Our first parents did not continue holy and happy. Being tempted by the devil, they transgressed God's law and fell into sin and misery. By their disobedience they lost the image and favor of God; they were consequently driven out of Eden, having become subject to pain and death.

Their sin not only injured themselves, but all their posterity, who were individually born in the image of fallen Adam, destitute of original righteousness, and under the wrath of God.

ANALYSIS.

Q. What doctrines are stated in this section?

A. 1. Man's fall from holiness by voluntary sin.
2. His consequent misery.
3. The universal prevalence of sin and its consequences among the descendants of Adam.

Explanatory and Practical Questions.

Q. Were Adam and Eve under any necessity of yielding to the temptation of the devil?

A. They were not; they had perfect freedom to obey or disobey God at their own choice.

Q. Who is the devil?

A. The chief of the fallen angels, who, before the creation of man, sinned against God, and were cast out of heaven.—Jude 6; 1 Pet. v, 8.

Q. What is the present state of those fallen angels?

A. They are reserved to the judgment of the great day.

Q. What is their employment?

A. Their employment is to tempt men to sin, and to lead them to their own place of misery.—Jude 6; 1 Pet. v, 8.

Q. Can they do what they please?

A. They cannot; God limits their power, and will save from their malice and subtilty all those who put their trust in him.—[James iv, 7; Luke xxii, 31, 32; Rom. xvi, 20.

Q. Are all wicked people then under the influence of Satan?

A. They are; for he leads them captive at his will.—2 Tim. ii, 26.

[RUM-DRAGON AND COLD-WATER ANGEL.]

Q. How does Satan tempt men to sin?

A. By putting evil thoughts and desires into their minds, to which they willingly yield.

Q. What preceded Adam's disobedience?

A. His disbelief of the word and threatening of God.

Q. What usually lies at the foundation of disobedience and sin against God?

A. Unbelief, or a want of faith.

Q. What reasons can you assign why man ought always to obey God?

A. God is his Creator, his Benefactor, and his rightful Governor.

Q. Why is it right and necessary that God should punish sin?

A. In order to vindicate his law, to preserve his authority, and to promote the greatest good of his creatures.

Q. What facts can you mention in proof of the universal depravity of man?

A. History and observation prove that in all times, places, and circumstances, men have been prone to sin and iniquity.

QUESTION FOR STUDY. *Does history give account of any nation or people who have been free from wars, contentions, and crimes?*

Definitions.

Transgress. To pass over, to break.
Prevalence. Existence and extension.
Voluntary. Of one's own choice.
Admonish. Warn.
Listen. To hear attentively.
Precede. To go before.
Foundation. That on which anything rests.
Benefactor. One who does good to another.
Governor. One who governs.
Depravity. Wickedness.
Vindicate. To sustain, rescue from reproach.

[THE CITY OF NAIN.]

IV. SALVATION.

§ 1.—SOURCE AND GROUNDS OF SALVATION.—Questions 37–44.

SUMMARY.

Q. On what grounds may we hope for salvation from the guilt and consequences of sin?

A. "God so loved the world, that he gave his only-begotten Son, that whosoever believeth in him should not perish, but have everlasting life."

Christ, therefore, took upon himself the form of a servant, and was made in the likeness of man. While in the flesh he gave an example of perfect goodness and holiness, that we might walk in his steps.

To offer to divine justice a full atonement for the sins of the world, he humbled himself, and became obedient unto death, even the death of the cross.

Having tasted death for every man, he rose

for our justification, and ascended to the right hand of God, where he ever liveth to make intercession for us.

ANALYSIS.

Q. What great Scripture truths are stated in this summary?

A. 1. God's love for the world.
2. His gift of his Son to die for human guilt.
3. Christ's humiliation.
4. Christ's perfect example.
5. Christ's atoning death for sinners.
6. His exaltation.
7. His intercession in our behalf.

Explanatory and Practical Questions.

Q. Was it possible for man to save himself from the guilt and consequences of sin?

A. It was wholly impossible. Man, being fallen and depraved, was unable to meet the current demands of the divine law, that is, to perform present duty, much less to make amends for past transgression.

Q. Who undertook, in our behalf, to offer the required satisfaction?

A. Jesus Christ, the Redeemer of mankind.

Q. What is redemption?

A. Redemption is that act of our Lord Jesus Christ, whereby satisfaction for sin is so far made to divine justice that man, on condition of repentance and faith, may be delivered from the guilt, power, pollution, and punishment of sin.

Q. How did the Lord Jesus Christ become our Redeemer?

A. By taking on him the nature of man, and offering himself a sacrifice for our sins.

Q. In what manner did Christ, being the Son of God, become man?

A. By taking to himself a true body and a soul, being conceived by the power of the Holy Ghost, and born of the Virgin Mary, but without sin.

Q. In what did Christ's humiliation consist?

A. In making himself of no reputation, and taking upon him the form of a servant, and being found in fashion as a man; in humbling himself and becoming obedient unto death, even the death of the cross.—Isa. liii, 3; Phil. ii, 7, 8.

Q. How did the death of Christ satisfy divine justice?

A. Having suffered for our sakes and in our stead, it enables Almighty God, consistently with his justice and holiness, to exercise his mercy in the forgiveness of sins.

Q. What attributes of God are specially harmonized and glorified in the death of Christ?

A. His justice and his love.

Q. With what sentiments ought we to reflect on the sufferings and death of Christ?

A. With deep convictions of the sinfulness of sin, by which Christ's humiliation and sufferings were occasioned; and with devout thanksgivings for God's unspeakable gift for our redemption.

[ACCUSATION OF CHRIST BEFORE PILATE.]

Q. In what does Christ's exaltation consist?

A. In his resurrection from the dead, in his ascension into heaven, in his sitting at the right hand of God the Father, and in his appointment to judge the world at the last day.—
[1 Cor. xv, 4; Mark xvi, 19; Acts xvii, 31.

Q. What offices does Christ fulfill as our Redeemer?

A. As our Redeemer, Christ has become our Prophet, Priest, and King.

Q. How does Christ execute the office of a Prophet?

A. In revealing to us, by his word and Spirit, the will of God for our salvation.—John i, 18; xx, 31; xiv, 26.

Q. How does Christ execute the office of a Priest?

A. In his having once offered up himself as a sacrifice to satisfy divine justice and to reconcile us to God, and in making continual intercession for us.—Heb. ix, 28; ii, 17; vii, 25.

Q. How does Christ execute the office of a King?

A. In subduing us to himself, and in ruling and defending us, and in restraining and conquering all his and our enemies.

Definitions.

Source. The origin.
Grounds. The basis.
Salvation. Deliverance from evil and sin.
Consequence. Necessary result.
Atonement. Propitiation.
Justification. Pardon and acceptance.
Intercession. Pleading for others.
Humiliation. Degradation, debasement.
Example. A pattern of life.
Exaltation. Elevation, glorification.
Infinite. Unlimited, pertaining to Deity.
Guilt. Wickedness.
Pollution. Defilement.
Punishment. Chastisement.
Meanness. Lowliness.
Poverty. Want, indigence.
Circumstances. Things surrounding.
Enduring. Suffering.
Despised. Contemptuously regarded.
Rejected. Cast off.
Satisfy. To meet the full demand of.
Deserve. To be worthy of.
Merit. Worth.
Stead. Place.
Forgiveness. Pardon.
Consistently. Properly, of right.
Harmonized. Made to agree.
Glorified. Made glorious.
Sentiments. Thoughts and feelings.
Conviction. Strong persuasion of mind.
Sinfulness. Wickedness, guilt.
Devout. Worshipful, heartfelt.
Unspeakable. Beyond the expression of language
Appointment. Commission.
Resurrection. Rising from the dead.
Prophet. An extraordinary teacher.
Priest. One who sacrifices and intercedes.
King. One that governs and protects his subjects.
Execute. Fulfill or perform.
Continual. Perpetual.
Reconcile. To restore to favor.
Subdue. Conquer.

§ 2.—CONDITIONS OF SALVATION.—Questions 45–53.

SUMMARY.

Q. Will you state what you know of the conditions of salvation?

A. Although Christ has died for all, yet men are not saved unconditionally, except infants and those who know not good and evil.

[THE JAILER AND THE APOSTLES.]

The conditions of salvation are *repentance* toward God, and *faith* toward our Lord Jesus Christ.

Repentance is a godly sorrow on account of sin, indicated by the forsaking of sin and a sincere turning to God.

Faith in Jesus Christ is the act of receiving and trusting in him alone for salvation. The power to repent and believe is freely given of God, and we may know when we are true believers in Christ by having the Spirit of God to bear witness with our spirit that we are the children of God.

ANALYSIS.

Q. What principal doctrines are stated in this section?

A. 1. That the salvation of infants, and of those who die without having voluntarily sinned, is secured by the atonement.

2. Repentance and faith are the essential conditions of salvation to all sinners.

3. The witness of the Spirit is the privilege of all true believers.

Explanatory and Practical Questions.

Q. What is the inevitable doom of those who die in sin, notwithstanding the atonement?

A. To go away into everlasting punishment.

Q. Whose fault will it be if any are finally lost?

A. Their own; since God has freely invited all men to come unto him and be saved.

Q. Is not the mercy of God amply justified in offering salvation to men on reasonable terms?

A. It is. Indeed, God could do no more to save them without interfering with their free moral agency.

Q. By what influences are men led to repentance?

A. By the gracious influences of the Holy Spirit?

Q. What states of mind are implied in repentance?

A. A sense of one's own sinfulness, and an apprehension of the mercy of God in Christ, together with grief, and hatred of sin, and a full purpose to turn from it to God.

Q. Can there be any repentance unto salvation, unaccompanied by a forsaking of sin?

A. There cannot. For "the sorrow of the world worketh death."—2 Cor. vii, 10.

Q. What are we to understand by the sorrow of the world?

A. Regret and grief on account of the consequences of sin, without any sincere purpose to amend one's life.

Q. Can any one be saved by repentance only?

A. "Without faith it is impossible to please God." "By grace are ye saved, through faith."—Heb. xi, 6; Eph. ii, 8.

Q. In what light therefore are we to regard repentance?

A. As a necessary preparation for, and antecedent to, evangelical faith.

Q. What is faith in general?

A. Faith in general is a conviction of the truth and reality of those things of which God has told us in the Bible.

Q. Can this faith save us?

A. It cannot; "the devils believe, and tremble."—[James ii, 19.

Q. What are the characteristics of saving faith?

A. A personal belief that Christ died for *me*, and a personal reliance on him alone, both now and forever, for salvation.

Q. What ought every believer to have as an evidence of his faith?

A. The double witness of his own spirit and the Spirit of God.

[COMMUNION WITH GOD.]

QUESTION FOR SELF-EXAMINATION.
Have you this faith?

Definitions.

Conditions. Terms.
Indicated. Shown.
Principal. Chief.
Inevitable. Unavoidable.
Interfering with. Influencing.
Consequences. Results.
Preparation. The act of making ready.
Unconditionally. Absolutely and without reference to terms.
Reliance. Confiding trust.
Witness. Testimony.
Voluntarily. Willfully, of choice.
Amply. Fully.
Apprehension. Perception.
Amend. Improve.
Antecedent. That which goes before.
Characteristics. Peculiar marks.
Conviction. Inward persuasion.

§ 3.—FRUITS AND EXTENT OF SALVATION.—Questions 54–61.

SUMMARY.

Q. What are the results of saving faith?

A. Justification, regeneration, and sanctification. *Justification* is that act of God's free grace in which he pardons our sins, and accepts us as righteous in his sight, for the sake of Christ.

Regeneration is the new birth of the soul in the image of Christ, whereby we become the children of God: and sanctification is that act of divine grace whereby we are made holy.

It is the privilege of every believer to be wholly sanctified, and to love God with all his heart in the present life; but at every stage of Christian experience there is danger of falling from grace, which danger is to be guarded against by watchfulness, prayer, and a life of faith in the Son of God.

ANALYSIS.

Q. What are the principal doctrines stated in this section?

A. 1. Justification.
2. Regeneration.
3. Sanctification.
4. The privilege of entire sanctification in this life.
5. The liability and danger of falling from grace.
6. The necessity of persevering in Christian faith and duty to the end of life.

Explanatory and Practical Questions.

Q. What particulars does the blessing of justification imply?

A. First, the forgiveness of our sins; second, our acceptance with God; third, our regeneration and adoption.

Q. What is implied in regeneration?

A. That great change which God works in the soul when he raises it from the death of sin to the life of righteousness, creating it anew in Christ Jesus after the image of God.

Q. What is adoption?

A. Adoption is an act of God's free grace, whereby, upon the forgiveness of sins, we are received into the number, and entitled to the privileges, of the sons of God.

[ANGELIC GUIDANCE.]

Q. What blessings in this life accompany our justification and adoption?

A. A sense of God's love, peace of conscience, joy in the Holy Ghost, and hope of the glory of God.

Q. Are not justification and regeneration very nearly identical?

A. Every one who is justified is also regenerated. Justification places us in a *new relation*, that of favor with God. Regeneration is a *new state*; that of being born again, or renewed in righteousness.

Q. What other term is used to signify the great change which every sinner must experience in order to enter heaven?

A. *Conversion*, which, implying a complete renewal of heart and life, comprehends justification, regeneration, and adoption.

Q. When is sanctification begun?

A. In regeneration, by which we receive power to grow in grace and in the knowledge of Christ, and to live in the exercise of inward and outward holiness.

Q. What is entire sanctification?

A. The state of being entirely cleansed from sin, so as to love God with all our heart, and mind, and soul, and strength, and our neighbor as ourselves.

Q. Should Christians who have attained this high state of grace pause in their career, as though there were no further improvement?

A. They should still grow in knowledge and in grace, and improve faster than before.

Q. In speaking of Christian perfection, do we imply absolute perfection, or that its possessor may not err?

A. Absolute perfection belongs not to men, nor to angels, but to God alone. No man is infallible while in the body.

Q. In what then does Christian perfection consist?

A. In perfect love.

Q. Why do we infer that even the highest state of grace may be lost, and its possessor perish at last?

A. Because the whole of life is a probation, and only they that endure to the end have the promise of being saved.

Q. Do the fruits of faith terminate with death?

A. They are only begun in the present life; for at death the souls of believers immediately pass into glory, while their bodies will rest in the grave till the resurrection.—Phil. i, 23; 1 Thess. iv, 14.

Q. What benefit will believers receive from Christ at the resurrection?

A. At the resurrection, believers, being raised up in glory, shall be openly acknowledged and accepted in the day of judgment, and made perfectly blessed in the full enjoyment of God to all eternity.—1 Cor. xv, 43; Matt. x, 32; 1 Thess. iv, 17.

Definitions.

Particulars. Several things.
Identical. The same.
Relation. Moral position.
Exercise. Practice.
Career. Onward course.
Infallible. Incapable of error.
Acknowledged. Publicly recognized.
Acceptance. State of favor.
State. Actual condition.
Comprehends. Embraces or includes.
Cleansed. Purified.
Absolute. Unlimited.
Probation. State of trial.
Immediately. At once.

[VIEW OF NABULUS.]

V. THE MEANS OF GRACE.

§ 1.—THE CHURCH AND MINISTRY.—Questions 62–67.

SUMMARY.

Q. What can you say of the Church and ministers of Christ?

A. The visible Church of Christ is a congregation of faithful men, in which the pure word of God is preached, and the sacraments duly administered according to Christ's ordinance. The whole body of God's true people, in every period of time, constitutes the invisible Church. All persons where the gospel is preached, ought to become believers in Christ, and members of his Church, in order to have a visible union with the Head of the Church, and communion with his people. For the establishment and extension of true religion, faithful men are called of God, and set apart by the Church to the office and work of the ministry.

ANALYSIS.

Q. What are the principal topics of this section?

A. 1. The visible Church of Christ.
2. The invisible Church.

3. The duty of membership in the Church.
4. The object and privileges of Church-membership.
5. The divine call of the ministry.
6. The work and office of the ministry.

Explanatory and Practical Questions.

Q. Has Christ in establishing his visible Church marked out any one essential form of organization and government?

A. He has not, but has evidently left the details of Church organization and government to his people in different ages and circumstances, subject to the general authority of the Scriptures.

Q. From what source may we derive the best instruction on the subject?

A. From the examples of the early Churches, as recorded in the New Testament.

Q. Can any particular Church apply to itself the term Catholic?

A. It cannot with propriety, for the essential meaning of that term is *general* or *universal*.

Q. How should you regard all attempts to appropriate the term Holy Catholic exclusively to any particular branch or sect of Christians.

A. As absurd and evil; absurd, because even granting that the Church pretending to be Catholic were a true and holy Church, its course would be like that of a single member of a body claiming to be the body; evil, because wrong in themselves, and calculated to foster superstition and intolerance.

Q. What must be considered essential to every true Christian Church?

A. The pure faith of the gospel, a holy ministry and membership, and a diligent practice of God's commands.

Q. What are the essential qualifications of every true minister of the Lord Jesus Christ?

A. A sincere faith in God's word, a genuine conversion, and a divine call to the work of saving souls.

Q. Is it right for a person not having been born again, nor having true faith toward our Lord Jesus Christ, to enter the Christian ministry?

A. Such an act should be considered sacrilegious, or a profane meddling with sacred things.

Q. What is a divine call to the ministry?

A. It is an act of the Holy Spirit, internally exciting a renewed person to take upon him the ministry of the gospel, for the glory of God and the salvation of men.

Q. Is an internal impression of such a duty sufficient?

A. It is not; it should be seconded by a corresponding voice of the Church.

Q. What offices do we recognize in the Christian ministry?

A. Those of deacons, elders, and bishops.

Q. What is the duty of a deacon?

A. To read and expound the word of God, to instruct the young, and to assist the elder in his work.

Q. What is the duty of an elder?

A. To preach the gospel, to administer the sacraments, and to exercise discipline in the Church.

[TEACHING THE YOUNG.]

Q. What is the duty of a bishop?

A. To oversee the spiritual and temporal interests of the Church, to preach the gospel, to ordain other ministers, and to direct their labors.

Q. Who were the apostles?

A. Those early ministers who had seen the Lord Jesus, and who were personally called, inspired, and commissioned by him to be the founders of his Church.

Q. When can a Church be considered apostolic?

A. When it has the apostolic doctrine, ministry, and worship, being built on the foundation of apostles and prophets, Christ himself being the Chief Corner-Stone.—Eph. ii, 20.

Q. Is there or can there be any succession to the apostolic office?

A. No; in the nature of the case that office ceased with the circumstances and occasion of its creation.

Q. What then is meant by the term apostolical succession?

A. Its only proper signification is, a succession of holy men in the faith and labors of the apostles; in other words, a spiritual succession of those who follow the apostles as they followed Christ.

Q. How is the term "apostolical succession" sometimes improperly used?

A. In the pretense of tracing an exclusive lineal descent of the office of the Christian ministry down through the Popes of Rome and the Bishops of England, and in this channel only.

Q. What evils grow out of the doctrine of lineal apostolical succession?

A. A spirit of intolerance, and a confidence in rites and ceremonies not justified by the word of God.

Q. What sentiments should the different branches of the Christian Church cherish toward each other?

A. Sentiments of respect and charity.

Q. What was the origin of the term Methodist?

A. It was first applied to the Wesleys, in England, in 1729, as a term of reproach and ridicule on account of their method and strictness in religious duty.

Q. What was the moral state of England at the time when the Wesleys arose?

A. The people in general were ignorant of the true nature of religion, and even ministers openly practiced sin.

Q. What distinguishing doctrines were preached by the Wesleys?

A. The guilt and total depravity of man, a present salvation by faith in Christ alone, and the direct witness of the Holy Spirit.

Q. What was the result of such preaching?

A. A great and glorious revival of religion, the subjects of which were generally called Methodists.

Q. Has this revival ceased?

A. No; its effects and benefits have come down to us, and thus the term Methodist has been perpetuated and made common.

[VISITING THE PRISONER.]

Q. Why is our Church also called Episcopal?

A. On account of its form of government, it being under the superintendence of bishops.

Q. What are some of the characteristics of the Methodist Episcopal Church?

A. Its evangelical doctrines, its itinerant ministry, and its peculiar means of grace, namely, love-feasts and class-meetings.

[A MISSIONARY AMONG THE INDIANS.]

Q. What is meant by the itinerancy?

A. A system of ministerial labor by which, annually, every itinerant minister is designated to labor in some proper field, and every field, as far as possible, furnished with a minister.

Q. Do ministers and members of the Methodist Episcopal Church enjoy as high and as complete spiritual immunities and advantages as any other Church or branch of the Church of Christ?

A. They undoubtedly do.

Q. What is a love-feast?

A. A meeting of Christians, at which bread and water are partaken of in token of brotherly love and in imitation of the early Christians, (Jude 12,) at which also narratives of Christian experience are given.

Q. What is a class-meeting?

A. A weekly meeting of a certain number of the members of the Church, one of whom is called the class-leader, for social worship and mutual religious improvement.

Definitions.

Visible. Capable of being seen.
Invisible. Impossible to be seen.
Establishment. Founding.
Extension. Spread.
Essential. Absolutely necessary.
Organization. Internal arrangement.
Government. Direction.
Example. Act to be imitated.
Appropriate. Claim as one's own.
Exclusively. Debarring all others.
Absurd. Without reason.
Qualifications. Tokens of fitness.
Superstition. False ideas of religion.
Intolerance. Want of charity, disposition to persecute.
Exciting. Moving.
Renewed. Converted.
Discipline. Government, correction.
Corresponding. Answering to.
Temporal. Relating to outward things.
Administer. Officially give.
Commissioned. Specially authorized.
Distinguishing. Peculiar.
Perpetual. Continued in use.
Superintendence. Official oversight.
Evangelical. In the spirit and truth of the gospel.
Itinerant. Traveling or moving from place to place.
Immunities. Peculiar privileges.
Narratives. Statements.
Advantages. Means of good or profit.

§ 2.—THE SACRAMENTS.—Questions 68–75.

SUMMARY.

Q. What can you say of the sacraments?

A. A sacrament is an outward and visible sign of an inward and spiritual grace.

There are two sacraments, baptism and the Lord's supper.

1. BAPTISM.

Q. What can you say of baptism?

A. Water, applied in the name of the Father, and of the Son, and of the Holy Ghost, is the outward sign in baptism, signifying the inward grace of a death unto sin and a new birth unto righteousness.

Baptized persons are admitted to the visible Church of Christ; and their relation to him as the Mediator of the new covenant, and their title to the spiritual blessings thereto belonging, are, by this sacrament, solemnly confirmed.

ANALYSIS.

Q. What are the principal topics of this section?

A. 1. The definition of a sacrament.
2. The outward sign in baptism.
3. The inward grace signified.
4. The advantages secured to baptized persons.
5. The obligations laid upon them.

Explanatory and Practical Questions.

Q. What is meant by an outward and visible sign?

A. Something which may be seen and applied to a purpose and in a meaning which in its own nature it has not.

Q. What is meant by an inward spiritual grace?

A. Some favor given us, whereby the state of our souls is made better.

Q. What is the water used in baptism designed to represent?

A. The blood of Christ, by which he washes us from our sins.—[Rev. i, 5; Heb. xii, 24; 1 Pet. i, 2.

Q. Is any particular mode of administering water in baptism enjoined in Scripture?

A. There is not; hence it is neither wise nor Scriptural to insist upon any mode as essential to valid baptism.

Q. What mode of baptism does our Church most commonly practice?

A. Sprinkling, as that for which we have the greatest number of Scripture examples and analogies.

Q. Is there any Scripture authority for making the sign of the cross in baptism?

A. There is not; and its use is only indicative of Romish superstition.

Q. What authority have we for baptizing infant children?

A. The practice of the apostles; and the command of Christ,

wherein he says, "Suffer the little children to come unto me, and forbid them not: for of such is the kingdom of God."— [Mark x, 14.

Q. What further authority?

A. Christ's commands: "Go ye into all the world, and preach the gospel to every creature." "Go ye, therefore, and teach

[SAILING OF A MISSIONARY SHIP.]

all nations, baptizing them in the name of the Father, and of the Son, and of the Holy Ghost." Which commands clearly include the young as well as the old.—Mark xvi, 15; Matt. xxviii, 19.

Q. What obligations were laid upon you in Christian baptism?

A. My baptism obliges me to renounce the devil and all his works, the pomp and vanity of this wicked world, and all the sinful lusts of the flesh; also to believe the whole faith of the gospel, and to keep God's holy will and commandments, walking in the same all the days of my life.

Q. Is it right to lay such obligations upon young children?

A. It is; for several reasons.

1. Because God himself makes these requirements of all his creatures.

2. Because they are under a natural and eternal obligation to love and serve God, independent of this covenant.

3. Because they are bound for their own good, and agreeably to the practice of mankind in other things.

Q. Ought not children to be carefully instructed in the nature and obligations of the baptismal covenant?

A. They ought; and as soon as they are capable, they ought to assume its pledges as their own.

Q. Will Christian baptism of itself save our souls?

A. It will not; unless we indeed become new creatures in Christ, and are created in him unto good works, we shall forfeit the benefits secured to us by baptism.—2 Cor. v, 17; Eph. ii, 10.

Q. Have we reason, then, to be grateful for this rite and ordinance of our holy religion?

A. We should indeed be grateful for it as a divinely-appointed means of enabling us to work out our salvation, and to lay hold on eternal life.

Definitions.

Signifying. Indicating.
Obligations. Incumbent duties.
Insist upon. Urgently require.
Renounce. Cast off, reject.
Independent of. Without reference to.
Instructed. Taught.
Ordinance. Divine institution.
Confirmed. Ratified or strengthened.
Represent. Show forth, or stand in place of.
Authority. Warrant, permission by Scripture precept or example.
Requirements. Demands.
Agreeably to. In conformity with.
Capable. Able.

[THE FOUNTAIN OF CANA.]

2. THE LORD'S SUPPER.

Q. What have you learned concerning the Lord's supper?

A. The sacrament of the Lord's supper was ordained for the continual remembrance of the sacrifice of Christ's death, and of the benefits that we thereby receive. The outward sign of the Lord's supper is bread and wine, received according to Christ's command. The inward grace of this sacrament is the communion of the body and blood of

Christ, whereby we are reminded of his sacrificial death, and spiritually strengthened to do his will.

ANALYSIS.

Q. What are the principal topics of this summary?

A. 1. The object of the Lord's supper.
2. The outward sign employed.
3. The inward spiritual grace signified and promoted.

Explanatory and Practical Questions.

Q. What do the symbols bread and wine used in the Lord's supper signify?

A. They represent, as solemn emblems, the body and blood of Christ.

Q. Did the Lord Jesus command that both should be received?

A. He did; and those who deny the cup to the laity, administer but half a sacrament.

Q. How should the body and blood of Christ be received by believers in the sacrament?

A. Spiritually, to the strengthening and refreshing of their souls.—1 Cor. x, 16; John vi, 54, 55.

Q. Are the souls of all persons who receive the consecrated elements of the Lord's supper refreshed and strengthened thereby?

A. No; very unworthy persons may partake of the bread and wine to their own condemnation, but true believers only secure the spiritual benefits of the sacrament.

Q. Who ought to partake of this holy sacrament?

A. All Christians, or persons who profess themselves followers of Christ, should receive the Lord's supper with true repentance and faith.

Q. Do not those persons professing Christianity act very wrong who neglect or refuse to receive the Lord's supper?

A. They are guilty of great ingratitude to God, who has offered them such a privilege; and they violate the express command of Christ, who said, "Do this in remembrance of me."

Q. What should be the habit of Christians in reference to the sacrament?

A. To receive it regularly and frequently, in obedience to the command of Christ.—Luke xxii, 19.

Q. What duty do they thus perform to the world?

A. They show forth and commemorate the Lord's death until he shall come again.—1 Cor. xi, 26.

Q. What duty toward God do we perform in this holy act?

A. We confess Christ, and declare our entire dependence upon his death as the only atonement for our sins, and as our only hope of salvation. We also declare our love and thankfulness to God for the gift of a Saviour, and our desire to enjoy communion with him and with our fellow-Christians in the remembrance of Christ's death.

Q. What is required of those who come to the Lord's supper?

A. To examine themselves whether they are in charity with all men; whether they truly repent of all their sins, steadfastly purposing to lead a new life; and whether they have a lively faith in God's word and grace.—1 Cor. xi, 28.

Q. What do you mean by a lively faith?

A. Such a faith as shows itself by works pleasing to God.—[James ii, 17, 18.

Q. If, on self-examination, persons find themselves destitute of the proper qualifications for receiving the holy sacrament, have they a good excuse for neglecting it?

A. By no means. Every one ought to have these qualifications; and no person who has them not, is fit for the kingdom of heaven.

Q. What should such persons do?

A. Immediately and earnestly seek the grace they need by all the appointed means.

Definitions.

Consecrated. Set apart to a holy use.
Confess. Publicly own.
Ordained. Divinely appointed.
Refreshing. Making vigorous.
Condemnation. Liability to punishment
Steadfastly. Earnestly and constantly.

[VIEW OF TIBERIAS.]

§ 3.—THE WORD OF GOD AND PRAYER.—Questions 76–84.

SUMMARY.

Q. What can you say of the word of God?

A. The word of God, as contained in the Scriptures of the Old and New Testaments, is called the Holy Bible. It is that revelation of divine truth and record of God's will, from which we derive all correct knowledge of religious truth and duty. It is the only sufficient rule of a Christian's faith and practice.

Q. What is prayer?

A. Prayer is the offering up of our desires unto God in the name of Christ. Prayer should always be accompanied with humble confession of sin, with hearty thanksgiving for God's mercies, and sincere faith in his promises. We should pray publicly in the house of God, socially in our families, and privately in our closets.

A special example of prayer is given us in Scripture, viz.: The Lord's Prayer.

ANALYSIS.

Q. What are the principal truths recognized in this section?

A. 1. That God has made a revelation to man.
2. That the Bible contains that revelation.
3. That the Scriptures are our only and sufficient guide to truth and duty.
4. The nature and duty of prayer.

ANALYSIS OF THE LORD'S PRAYER.

Preface. Our Father which art in heaven.

Petition 1. Hallowed be thy name.
2. Thy kingdom come.
3. Thy will be done in earth as it is in heaven.
4. Give us this day our daily bread.
5. And forgive us our trespasses, as we forgive them that trespass against us.
6. And lead us not into temptation, but deliver us from evil.

Doxology. For thine is the kingdom, and the power, and the glory, forever. Amen.

Explanatory and Practical Questions.

Q. How are we to use the word of God?

A. By frequently and seriously reading and hearing it, with prayer to God that his Holy Spirit may show us its meaning, and apply it to our hearts.—John v, 39; Rom. x, 17.

Q. With what disposition of mind ought we to read and hear God's holy word?

A. With a meek and teachable disposition; with faith, and an intention to practice it by God's grace.—James i, 21; Matt. xi, 25; Heb. iv, 2; John vii, 17.

Q. Ought we not often to think upon what we have heard and read?

A. We ought to lay up the word of God in our hearts, and meditate thereon day and night.—Psa. cxix, 11; Luke ii, 19.

Q. To whom alone should we pray?

A. To Almighty God.

Q. How are we to regard prayer to images, saints, and the Virgin Mary?

A. As idolatry, and forbidden by God's command.

Q. Is the duty of prayer confined to any class of persons?

A. Prayer is a universal duty, required of every human being.

Q. What habits should Christians observe with reference to prayer?

A. They should pray frequently, regularly, and fervently.—1 Thess. v, 17; Psa. lv, 17; Phil. iv, 6.

Q. With what should we always accompany our prayer, both public and private?

A. With confession of our sins, and a thankful acknowledgment of God's mercies.

Q. Do we rightly use the Lord's Prayer when we content ourselves with merely repeating its form?

A. We ought to strive to fully comprehend its meaning, and to offer it with our hearts as well as our lips.

Q. What is the preface or invocation of our Lord's Prayer?

A. "Our Father which art in heaven."

Q. In what sense do we here address God as our Father?

A. As the Father and Creator of all things; as the Father of our Lord Jesus Christ; and especially as the Father of all true Christians, or "children of God."

Q. In what ways does God act toward us as our Father?

A. By his care in preserving us, by his goodness in aiding us, by his authority in correcting us, by his mercy in forgiving us, and by his love in providing for our present and eternal happiness.

*Q. Why should an individual say "*OUR *Father" instead of* MY *Father?*

A. That he may be reminded that God is the Father of others as well as himself. We have all one Father.—Mal. ii, 10.

Q. How then ought we to treat all men, and especially all Christians?

A. We ought to treat them as brethren.

["ALL YE ARE BRETHREN."]

Q. Why do we add "who art in heaven?"

A. To declare God's greatness and dominion: for "the Lord hath prepared his throne in the heavens, and his kingdom ruleth over all."—Psa. ciii, 19.

Q. What is the first petition in the Lord's Prayer?

A. "Hallowed by thy name."

Q. What does "hallowed" mean?

A. Hallowed means honored, reverenced, sanctified.

Q. What does the "name" of God principally denote?

A. The name of God represents his attributes, his authority, and his true religion.

Q. What, then, do we ask in this first petition?

A. We pray that God may be everywhere known and adored, his authority obeyed, and his religion embraced.

Q. When do we hallow God's name?

A. When we never use it profanely or triflingly; but when we worship God truly, and serve him faithfully.

Q. What is the second petition?

A. "Thy kingdom come."

Q. What is the purport of this petition?

A. That the kingdom of God may prevail and be established, and that the kingdom of Satan, sin, and death may be destroyed.

Q. Of what does God's kingdom consist?

A. The kingdom of his power, his grace, and his glory.

Q. What should we pray for concerning the first?

A. That, as God ruleth over all creatures, he would order all things for the glory of his name and the good of his people.

Q. What is the kingdom of grace?

A. It is that whereby God rules in the hearts of his children by his word and Spirit; and we pray that it may prevail universally, dispelling darkness and sin.

Q. What is the kingdom of glory?

A. It is that final triumph of God's power and grace for which the Christian longs in his anticipation of heaven, and of which he desires all men to become the subjects.

Q. What is the third petition?

A. "Thy will be done on earth as it is in heaven."

Q. What is comprehended in this request?

A. Universal obedience to God.

Q. What should be our great and constant business in this world?

A. To do God's holy will.

Q. How should we do it?

A. Cheerfully and perfectly, (by his assisting grace,) as the angels do it in heaven.

Q. With what should we accompany our prayers for the coming of God's kingdom and the doing of his will?

A. With zealous labors to promote both throughout the world.

Q. To what general subject do the first three petitions relate?

A. To the worship and service of God.

Q. To what do the three following relate?

A. To the supply of human wants—those of the body and the soul.

Q. What is the fourth petition, or that relating to our bodily wants?

A. "Give us this day our daily bread."

Q. What does this petition comprehend and teach?

A. It comprehends not merely our food, but all other things necessary for our subsistence and comfort; and teaches our constant dependence upon God for what we need or enjoy.

["LEAD US NOT INTO TEMPTATION."]

Q. To what do the fifth and sixth petitions relate?

A. To the wants of the soul, which are: forgiveness of sins, protection against temptation, and deliverance from evil.

Q. What does the fifth petition imply?

A. That we have sinned against God, and need his pardoning mercy.

Q. What does this petition also teach?

A. That we should forgive those who injure us as freely and as fully as we hope to be forgiven.

Q. What is the sixth petition?

A. "Lead us not into temptation, but deliver us from evil."

Q. What is the meaning of temptation?

A. A dangerous trial or enticement to sin.

Q. By what are men tempted to sin?

A. By the devil, who is called the tempter; by wicked people; and by their own bad passions.

Q. What alone can preserve us against injury by temptation and the evils that are in the world?

A. God's gracious power.

Q. Should we, in offering this petition, contemplate merely a deliverance from sin and wickedness in this life?

A. We should also supplicate deliverance from the consequence and punishment of sin in the world to come.

Q. What is the concluding sentence of the Lord's Prayer?

A. It is called the doxology, or praise to God. "For thine is the kingdom, and the power, and the glory, forever."

Q. What should it teach us?

A. That in all our prayers we should ascribe to God the honor due to his holy name.

Q. What is the meaning of the word Amen?

A. Amen signifies verily, truly, or "so let it be;" and at the end of our prayers, expresses a hearty wish that what we have asked for may be granted or accomplished.

Q. Are we to content ourselves with using only the Lord's Prayer?

A. The Lord's Prayer is general in its nature, and only designed to give us general instruction as to the manner and nature of prayer.

Q. Are we permitted to ask God for whatever we want?

A. In subjection to God's will, we are invited to "come boldly to the throne of grace;" and promised, that "whatsoever we ask in prayer, believing, we shall receive."—Heb. iv, 16; Matt. xxi, 22.

Definitions.

Revelation. Publication of what was before secret or unknown.
Sufficient. Nothing wanting.
Teachable. Disposed to be taught.
Intention. Purpose, design.
Meditate. Carefully reflect.
Comprehend. Understand.
Dispelling. Driving away.
Deliverance. The act of being set free.
Enticement. Attraction, allurement.
Contemplate. Desire, expect.
Supplicate. Pray for.

[ENTRANCE OF GAZA.]

VI. GOD'S LAW.

DUTIES TO GOD AND MAN.—QUESTIONS 85–103.

SUMMARY.

Q. What defines our chief duties to God and man?

A. The moral law of God, as contained in the ten commandments.

ANALYSIS.

Q. How may the moral law be divided?

A. 1. Into two tables.
2. Into ten precepts.
3. Into negative precepts and affirmative precepts.

Explanatory and Practical Questions.

Q. What is sometimes denominated the first table of the law?

A. The first four commandments taken collectively, which express our duty toward God.

Q. What is, in this distinction, the second table?

A. The last six commandments, which define our duties toward our fellow-beings.

Q. What is the force of a negative commandment?

A. It forbids every sort and degree of the sin it condemns, and enjoins the contrary duty.

Q. What is the force of an affirmative commandment?

A. It enjoins every sort and degree of the duty it expresses, and forbids the contrary sin.

Q. How many of the ten commandments are negative?

A. Eight: showing the great tendencies men have to evil when without divine restraint.

Q. What is the purport of the first commandment, "Thou shalt have no other gods before me?"

A. The first commandment concerns the acknowledgment and worship of God, and forbids:

1. The sin of atheists, who acknowledge no God.
2. The sin of the heathen, and those who serve false gods.
3. The sin of those who neglect to serve and worship the true God. It also enjoins our supreme worship of the one only and true God, whom we should love, fear, trust, and obey, above all others.

[IMAGE OF NEBUCHADNEZZAR.]

Q. What is the purport of the second commandment?

A. The second commandment concerns the worship of idols and false gods, which it forbids in every possible form, threatening judgment upon those who practice it, and promising mercy to all who love and obey God.

Q. What is the purport of the third commandment?

A. It concerns the name and honor of God, and, in spirit, forbids:

1. Irreverent thoughts of God.
2. Profanity, angry or trifling mention of God's name.
3. Blasphemy, or speaking evil of God's name or attributes.

4. Perjury, or false swearing.

It also enjoins, by inference, a reverent and devout use of the name of Jehovah.

Q. What is the purport of the fourth commandment?

A. The fourth commandment concerns the right use of time; it enjoins the holy employment or sanctification of one day in every week, and diligent labor during the other six days.

Q. Why is the first day of the week observed by Christians as the Sabbath; and not the seventh day, as by the Jews?

A. To commemorate the resurrection of Christ, after which event the first day of the week was called the Lord's day, and hallowed by the disciples and Christians.

Q. Does this change of the Sabbath from the seventh to the first day of the week interfere with the original commandment?

A. It does not; since that commandment evidently relates more to the portion of time which should be hallowed than to the particular day of the week which should be observed.

Q. What are forbidden on the holy Sabbath to all persons and families?

A. All worldly pleasures, and all labors and engagements, except works of necessity and mercy.—Mark ii, 25-28; Luke xiii, 16.

Q. What duties are enjoined?

A. God's day is to be kept holy by his public and private worship, by prayer, by alms-giving, by receiving and dispensing his word, and by meditating upon his glorious works in creation and redemption.

Q. What is the purport of the fifth commandment?

A. The fifth commandment concerns human relations, enjoining parental authority and filial honor; which implies love, reverence, obedience, support, and comfort from all children to their parents.

Q. What other duties are taught in this commandment, at least by inference?

A. The reciprocal duties of superiors and inferiors; for example, rulers, magistrates, ministers, masters, and those who are subject to them, and also the mutual duties of husbands and wives.

Q. How is this commandment distinguished by an apostle?

A. It is called "the first commandment with promise."—[Eph. vi, 2, 3.

Q. What is the purport of the sixth commandment?

A. The sixth commandment concerns the sacredness of human life.

It forbids murder and all passions and desires leading to that crime, such as anger, hatred, intemperance, and violent words or actions.

It also enjoins a proper care for the preservation of our own lives and the lives of our fellow-beings.

Q. What is the purport of the seventh commandment?

A. The seventh commandment concerns purity of life and chastity of conduct.

It forbids lasciviousness or impure thoughts, looks, actions, and words, together with fornication, adultery, and unlawful marriage.

It also enjoins, as necessary to keeping its spirit, chastity and modesty in thoughts, behavior, and apparel, and also sobriety and watchfulness.

Q. What is the purport of the eighth commandment?

A. The eighth commandment relates to the rights of property, and forbids all fraud, robbery, oppression, and theft, or taking what is not our own, whether great or small.

Q. What is the purport of the ninth commandment?

A. The ninth commandment concerns truth and man's good

name. It forbids lies, jealousies, slander, (*i. e.*, the raising or circulating of false or malicious reports,) and all false speaking or swearing; while it enjoins truthfulness at all times, and charitable feelings and words toward, and of, our fellow-men.

Q. What is the purport of the tenth commandment?

A. The tenth commandment concerns human desires and the thoughts of our hearts.

It forbids lust and covetousness of every kind and degree, and teaches us to regulate our affections, to restrain sinful desires, and to be content with what we have.

Q. In what way does our Saviour teach us that we are to keep these important commandments with reference to God and our neighbor?

A. By LOVE, which is the fulfilling of the law.—Rom. xiii, 10.

Q. Is it possible for us to love God as we ought while the heart is yet carnal?

A. It is not; and hence we see the necessity of a change of heart, or of being born again.

Q. What is the sum of your duty toward God?

A. My duty toward God is to believe in him, to fear him, and to love him with all my heart, with all my mind, with all my soul, and with all my strength; to worship him, to give him thanks, to put my whole trust in him, to call upon him, to honor his holy name, his Sabbath, and his word, and to serve him truly all the days of my life.

Q. What is your duty toward your neighbor?

A. My duty toward my neighbor is to love him as myself, and to do to all men as I would that they should do unto me; to love, honor, and succor my father and mother; to honor and obey my civil rulers; to submit myself to all my governors, teachers, spiritual pastors, and masters; to hurt nobody by word or deed; to be true and just in all my dealings; to bear no malice nor hatred in my heart; to keep my hands from stealing or taking what belongs to another, and my tongue from evil-speaking, lying, and slandering; to keep my body in temperance, soberness, and chastity; not to covet or desire other men's goods, but to learn and labor honestly to get my own living, and to do my duty in that state of life into which it shall please God to call me.

Q. Did our Saviour make any additions to the ten commandments?

A. Our Saviour, besides making numerous explanations and applications of God's moral law, said, "A new commandment I give unto you, That ye love one another."—John xiii, 34.

Q. What does this new commandment mean?

A. This new commandment means that we should not only

love our neighbor as ourselves, but that we should bear a particular affection for all those who are the disciples of Christ.—[Eph. vi, 24; 1 John iv, 11; iii, 16.

Q. Does not St. James teach us that if we break but one of the commandments, we shall fall into condemnation?

A. He does. "For whosoever shall keep the whole law, and yet offend in one point, he is guilty of all."—James ii, 10.

Q. Does not our Lord show us whom we are to understand by our neighbors, and whom we are commanded to love as ourselves?

A. He does. In the parable of the good Samaritan, he teaches us that every man of every nation is our neighbor, and that if any be in distress, we are bound to help and relieve them.

[RELIEVING THE AFFLICTED.]

Q. Has not our Lord given us another important precept founded upon our love to our neighbor?

A. He has. "Whatsoever ye would that men should do to you, do ye even so to them: for this is the law and the prophets."—[Matt. vii, 12.

Q. Has he not also given us certain rules to direct us in our conduct toward our enemies?

A. He has. "I say unto you, Love your enemies, bless them that curse you, do good to them that hate you, and pray for them which despitefully use you, and persecute you."—Matt. v, 44.

[THE GOOD SAMARITAN.]

Q. How does our Lord direct us to behave toward them who have injured us?

A. We are commanded to forgive them.—Matt. vi, 15.

Q. Does not the law of God, as explained and enlarged in the New Testament, contain various commands as to our tempers and dispositions?

A. It does: that we ought to be meek and lowly; patient under sufferings; and kind to all men.

Matt. xi, 29. Learn of me: for I am meek.

Luke xxi, 19. In your patience possess ye your souls.

Gal. vi, 10. As we have, therefore, opportunity, let us do good unto all men.

Q. Does it not contain various precepts as to our conduct in the different relations of life?

A. It does. 1. As to husbands and wives.

Eph. v, 25. Husbands, love your wives, even as Christ also loved the Church, and gave himself for it.

Eph. v, 22. Wives, submit yourselves unto your own husbands, as unto the Lord.

2. As to parents and children.

Eph. vi, 4. Fathers, provoke not your children to wrath; but bring them up in the nurture and admonition of the Lord.

Eph. vi, 1. Children, obey your parents in the Lord; for this is right.

3. As to masters and servants.

1 Pet. ii, 18. Servants, be subject to your masters with all fear; not only to the good and gentle, but also to the froward.

Col. iv, 1. Masters, give unto your servants that which is just and equal; knowing that ye also have a Master in heaven.

4. As to obedience to magistrates and governors.

Rom. xiii, 1. Let every soul be subject unto the higher powers. For there is no power but of God; the powers that be are ordained of God.

1 Pet. ii, 17. Honor all men; love the brotherhood; fear God; honor the king.

5. As to ministers of the gospel.

Heb. xiii, 17. Obey them that have the rule over you, and submit yourselves: for they watch for your souls, as they that must give account.

Q. To what end serveth the law of God?

A. The law of God serveth, in the first place, as the rule of our conduct: and in the second, to convince us of sin; for "by the law is the knowledge of sin."—Rom. iii, 20.

Rom. iii, 23. All have sinned, and come short of the glory of God.
Psa. xix, 12. Who can understand his errors?

Q. Are all transgressions of the law equally great?

A. Some sins in themselves, and by reason of several aggravations, are more heinous in the sight of God than others.—[John xix, 11.

Q. What does every sin deserve?

A. Every sin deserves God's wrath and curse, both in this life and that which is to come.—Gal. iii, 10; Rom. vi, 23.

Q. Does the law of God promise the pardon of sin to those who have transgressed it?

A. It does not: pardon is promised only in the gospel, through faith in our Lord Jesus Christ.

Q. Then must all who do not repent of their sins, and believe in Christ, as before explained, remain forever under the curse and vengeance of this just and holy law?

A. Certainly: for "he that believeth not shall be damned."—[Mark xvi, 16.

Q. But might you not obtain forgiveness by repenting, and keeping the law of God in future?

A. This I am not able to do without the grace of Christ; for "they that are in the flesh cannot please God." But if I could, present obedience cannot atone for my past sins, every one of which lays me under the curse of the law.—Rom. viii, 8.

Q. Well, then, trusting in the merits of Christ, as a helpless, guilty, and undone sinner, will you obtain the remission of your sins; and being regenerated by the Holy Spirit, will you be enabled by his help thenceforward to please God, and keep his commandments?

A. I shall: "For what the law could not do in that it was

weak through the flesh, God sending his own Son in the likeness of sinful flesh, and for sin, condemned sin in the flesh; that the righteousness of the law might be fulfilled in us, who walk not after the flesh, but after the Spirit."—Rom. viii, 3, 4.

Definitions.

Denominated. Named or called.
Affirmative. That which states or enjoins.
Negative. That which forbids.
Enjoins. Commands.
Irreverent. Lacking reverence or respect.
Commemorate. Perpetuate the remembrance of.
Dispensing. Administering.
Reciprocal. Mutual.
Preservation. Continued protection.
Malicious. Evil or injurious.
Covetousness. The sin of coveting.
Regulate. Govern.
Carnal. In a state of nature.
Succor. Aid, assist.
Precepts. Commands.
Transgression. Infractious disobedience.
Heinous. Culpable.
Vengeance. Just retribution.
Aggravations. Increased provocations.

[MOSQUE OF DAVID.]

VII. DEATH, JUDGMENT, AND ETERNITY.

QUESTIONS 104–112.

SUMMARY.

Q. What is the sum of your knowledge respecting death, the judgment, and eternity?

A. Life is short and uncertain, and we all must die. Death is a fearful thing to all but true Christians. They should not fear to die, because from them the sting of death is removed, and they know that they shall go to heaven. The bodies of men shall lie in the grave until the last day, when Christ shall come to raise the dead for judgment. There shall be a resurrection of the dead, both of the just and of the unjust, when we must all appear before the judgment seat of Christ, that every one may receive the things done in his body according to what he hath done, whether it be good or bad. Christ will then pronounce sentence on the wicked: "Depart from me, ye cursed, into everlasting fire, prepared for the devil and his angels." And to the righteous he will say:—"Come, ye blessed of my Father, inherit the kingdom prepared for you from the foundation of the world." Then the world shall be destroyed by fire, and the wicked shall go away into everlasting punishment, but the righteous into life eternal.

ANALYSIS.

Q. What separate doctrines are herein taught?

A. 1. The shortness and uncertainty of life.
2. The certainty of death.
3. The terror of death to the wicked.
4. The triumph of the righteous over death and the grave.
5. The resurrection of the dead.
6. The final judgment.
7. The destruction of the earth by fire.
8. The eternal punishment of the wicked.
9. The eternal happiness of the righteous.

Explanatory and Practical Questions.

Q. Of what great duty should we never lose sight?

A. Our duty to prepare for death and the judgment.

Q. Ought this preparation to make us sad or gloomy?

A. By no means. Religion is the source of all true and consistent cheerfulness.

Q. Is there no exception to the personal duty of each one to prepare to meet his God?

A. There is no exception. "Every one of us shall give account of himself to God."—Rom. xiv, 12.

Q. May every one of us be assured of mercy through the blood of the everlasting covenant?

A. Christ tasted death for every man; and "he is able to save them to the uttermost that come unto God by him."—[Heb. ii, 9; vii, 25.

Q. What then is our manifest duty?

A. To seek God while he may be found, and to call upon him while he is near.—Isa. lv, 6.

Q. What urgent motive should quicken us to repentance, faith, and all Christian duty?

A. Fear, lest a promise being left us of entering into rest, any of us should seem to come short of it.—Heb. iv, 1.

Q. What are we to dread in case of final impenitence and unfaithfulness?

A. A portion among hypocrites and unbelievers, in the place prepared for the devil and his angels, where their worm dieth not, and their fire is not quenched.

Q. What may we anticipate if obedient to the commands of God and faithful to his grace?

A. We may look forward to a companionship with saints, and angels, and glorified spirits, and our Redeemer, in heaven.

[FAINTING GRIEF.]

Q. What if we should be called upon to suffer persecution and sorrow in this life, on account of our bearing the cross of Christ?

A. "Our light affliction, which is but for a moment, worketh for us a far more exceeding and eternal weight of glory."—2 Cor. iv, 17.

Q. What then should be our earnest and constant resolve?

A. To give diligence to make our calling and election sure; so that an entrance may be ministered unto us abundantly into the everlasting kingdom of our Lord and Saviour Jesus Christ.—
[2 Pet. i, 10, 11.

Definitions.

Pronounce. Declare.
Quenched. Put out, extinguished.
Cheerfulness. Happy state of mind.
Anticipate. Expect.

[A DREAM OF HEAVEN.]

The End.

www.ingramcontent.com/pod-product-compliance
Lightning Source LLC
LaVergne TN
LVHW021404110826
845150LV00007B/1774